DRONES IN EDUCATION

Let Your Students' Imaginations Soar

Christopher Carnahan, Laura Zieger, Kimberly Crowley

International Society for Technology in Education
EUGENE, OREGON • ARLINGTON, VIRGINIA

Drones in Education
Let Your Students' Imaginations Soar
Christopher Carnahan, Laura Zieger, Kimberly Crowley

Editor: *Emily Reed*
Production Manager: *Christine Longmuir*
Copy Editor: *Jen Weaver-Neist*
Editorial Assistant: *Corinne Gould*
Book Design and Production: *Kim McGovern*

Library of Congress Cataloging-in-Publication Data available.

First Edition
ISBN: 978-1-56484-383-8
Ebook version available.

Printed in the United States of America

ISTE® is a registered trademark of the International Society for Technology in Education.

About ISTE

The International Society for Technology in Education (ISTE) is the premier nonprofit organization serving educators and education leaders committed to empowering connected learners in a connected world. ISTE serves more than 100,000 education stakeholders throughout the world.

ISTE's innovative offerings include the ISTE Conference & Expo, one of the biggest, most comprehensive ed tech events in the world—as well as the widely adopted ISTE Standards for learning, teaching and leading in the digital age and a robust suite of professional learning resources, including webinars, online courses, consulting services for schools and districts, books, and peer-reviewed journals and publications. Visit iste.org to learn more.

Related ISTE Titles

Getting Started with LEGO Robotics, by Mark Gura

To see all books available from ISTE, please visit iste.org/resources

About the Authors

Christopher Carnahan, PhD is the doctoral program coordinator and assistant professor in the Educational Technology Department at New Jersey City University. His research centers on the implementation of innovative technologies such as drones, robotics, and virtual learning environments to improve student engagement and achievement. Carnahan provides consulting and professional development services to K–12 districts on how to successfully implement emerging technologies. His website is www.cdcarnahan.com

Laura Zieger, PhD is the chairperson and a professor in the Department of Educational Technology at New Jersey City University. Her research interests include transformation of learning with emerging technologies including robotics, immersive virtual environments and drones, online teaching, and social computing applications in education. Zieger has published widely and her research and involvement in online parenting communities has been published in Family PC magazine and Sesame Street Parents. She is an invited speaker to schools and organizations.

Kimberly Crowley is mathematics supervisor for a large urban school district in New Jersey. She encourages implementation of STEM and STEAM initiatives within her district. Her goal is to guide administrators and teachers to use technology as part of project-based learning to improve student engagement.

Contents

Foreword

From agriculture to logistics and cinematography to workplace management, unmanned autonomous systems—including unmanned aerial vehicles (UAVs)—are poised to alter the way work is done. These machines represent a sea change in how humans interact with technology. We colloquially refer to them as "drones," but they are nothing like the worker bees or weapons of warfare that they may be associated with. It would be more accurate to view them as flying robots that utilize the same engineering principles that have made smart phones ubiquitous.

I have been passionate about drones for many years and as a community leader, visual artist, and STEM instructor, I have found that the power in their potential bridges gaps of age, demography, gender, and occupation. I often refer to myself as an "accidental advocate." I didn't set out to become a spokesperson for a cause, but in my role as president of the Drone User Group Network (DUGN), I have advocated for the safe and responsible civilian use of drone technology and have made lifelong affiliations, friends, and colleagues among the 20,000 people (and growing) in our global network. As a photographer and filmmaker, drones scratch an itch that I can only describe as the point where art and science intersect. It is both thrilling and satisfying to operate a drone and understand why and how it functions. I never thought I could get excited about feedback loops or differential equations, but here I am sharing these very concepts with students of all ages in community outreach programs and structured school programs.

Drones are engaging educational tools, as evidenced by their increasing popularity in schools. I have yet to hear a student claim lack of interest when given the opportunity to learn about what drones can do and, more importantly, what they can do with drones. Principles of physics, aeronautics, radio frequency theory, geographical information systems, and lens-based media collection, are all well within the grasp of our students in their exploration of drone technology. The drone is a means to engaging higher learning, and with the information provided in this book, you will be able to capably drones into your instruction and instill your students with a passion for emerging technologies.

> — *Steven Cohen*
> President Drone User Group Network (dugn.org)
> UAS/Mechatronics Instructor
> Bergen County Technical Schools
> Applied Technology High School
> Paramus, NJ

Introduction

"You are the coolest teacher in the school!"

That's what you are going to hear when you walk into the classroom. Simply by purchasing this book, you have demonstrated your level of coolness. Who doesn't want to fly an unmanned aircraft with remote video and photographic capabilities? And who wouldn't want to see the wonder on students' faces as they fly a drone and apply the concepts learned? The answer is a no-brainer.

This book was written for educators who want to incorporate drones into their curriculum but have no idea where to start. It will cover all that you need to know to get off of the ground (puns are intentional!) with a drone program in your school. It covers such basic but important information as which drones need to be registered and where you can fly them. It also provides recommendations as to the drones that are best for specific age levels and subject areas. The information provided here will offer you everything you need to know to start using drones in the classroom.

When incorporating a new cutting-edge technology into any school setting, you need to know whether it is useful. You do not want to undertake the time and expense of incorporating drones if there is not support that they will have an impact on teaching and learning.

So, the organization of the book is logical. Chapter 1 discusses the rationale for using drones in education and offers data to support your goals. You might want to quote the research here to support your budget proposal or curriculum unit, for example.

In Chapter 2, you will learn about other teachers like yourself who have successfully integrated drones into their classroom teaching. Their stories will inspire you and dissuade your fears about this undertaking. When you see the smiles and enthusiasm on the faces of your students, you will know that it is all worthwhile.

Chapter 3 gets into the nitty-gritty of the laws and ethical issues surrounding drones. You've probably heard stories in the news about drone crashes in football stadiums and regulations about pilot licenses. This chapter covers the policies and rules as they pertain to teachers and the use of drones in education. Your principal will be happy to know that you understand the rules and laws, and have complied with all federal and state regulations.

This book will also help you to determine which drone is right for you and your school. Not all drones are created equal. While the more expensive drones have more capabilities, you might find that a less expensive and smaller version is better suited to your needs. Chapter 4 discusses how drones work in different settings (classroom, gymnasium, playground) and which drones are best for varying ages and technical expertise.

And what about the big question: how do you fly a drone and, more importantly, teach students to fly? If you have never flown a drone, do not worry. There are spider drones that are perfect for you. Chapters 4 and 5 offer tips to get you up and running, and troubleshooting tricks for when you are not. Both chapters focus on selecting the right drone and keeping them operational. A drone is not worth anything if it is not flying!

Once you have mastered flying, the work begins: integrating drones in the curriculum. In Chapter 5, we discuss classroom implementation through our SOAR (safety, operation, active learning, and research) model. SOAR is a conceptual model to provide teachers with the technical and theoretical knowledge they need to include drone and robotic technology in their classrooms, and to engage learners. It offers a simple formula to ensure safe operation and maximize engagement and learning in every classroom.

A key element of the SOAR model is to provide a curriculum-based program that excites students in STEM (science, technology, engineering, and math) pathways. Unmanned aerial vehicles (UAVs) offer the ideal tool for developing invaluable STEM skills, and Chapter 6 translates what teachers learn about UAVs into sample lesson plans for the classroom and across the curriculum. You can improve learning by utilizing hands-on activities with current technology; this chapter helps you to get started with some of the tested ideas that have worked for other teachers in their classrooms. Once you get the hang of using drones and understanding the proficiencies they offer, the sky is the limit.

Finally, the last chapter discusses some of the uses of drones in the real world. While this may not be directly applicable to your classroom, it is important for students to be prepared for careers in our technologically advanced society. Chapter 7 provides guidance for teachers who will undoubtedly be asked how students can continue working with drones in their future.

We hope you enjoy the book, but one outcome is guaranteed: if you have not already, you will win the title of the coolest teacher in the school.

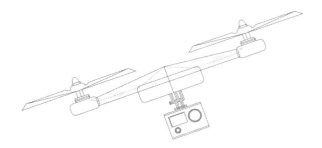

CHAPTER 1

Learning and Teaching in the Digital Age

Have you ever watched teenagers playing an intense video game—yelling and cheering, high-fiving each other over a clever play or strategy? Surely you have observed teenagers texting their friends while standing in a tight circle, heads down and giggling?

Engagement and Motivation

The focus on technology by children today is so unwavering that most adults are frustrated by it. How often do you hear parents saying, "Put the phone down," or teachers warning students to "put the phone away before it is confiscated"?

Yet most adults have watched in awe as toddlers pick up their parents' cell phones and play digital games. As adults in a generation that had to learn technology, it may be difficult sometimes to understand these children who are growing up with technology in every facet of their lives. Their brains have become wired to learn how to use technology with little or no instruction.

Now imagine schools where students are engaged in learning every subject because they want to, not because they have to. You would witness students collaborating about the subject matter in important and meaningful ways. They would be testing hypotheses involved in hands-on projects using the latest technology tools—that is the picture most people imagine when they are asked to envision the ideal classroom.

Ask those same people to paint the picture of the actual classroom today and it will likely be very different. The traditional teacher-centered method of instruction is often depicted as students sitting in rows of desks while reading textbooks and taking handwritten notes about the topic. Most assessments are given in the textbooks publisher's format to all students, perhaps utilizing Scantron standardized tests, and then students wait a few days to receive their scores. Sometimes, the test is not returned for students to see what they got wrong and, more importantly, why their answers were wrong. Consider the famous classroom scene from the movie *Ferris Bueller's Day Off* ("Anyone…? Anyone…?"), and you get the idea.

The two scenes representing a traditional teacher-centered classroom and a technology-rich, student-centered classroom are two widely different approaches to learning the same subject. The challenge with school today is not the content being taught but the manner in which it is being delivered. The difficulty for most educators is finding a way to deliver curriculum content packaged in a digital wrapper. Student-centered, technology-driven learning has become a major cornerstone of digital-age education. Readily available technology delivers access to global resources and supports educators in addressing the wide-ranging needs of their diverse learners. Technology-assisted instruction provides resources far beyond the means of traditional classroom instruction by enabling students and teachers to access and share multimedia information. However, while all of this opportunity exists, accessing and utilizing it requires time and money—two things most schools and teachers do not have in excess.

The depiction of most workplaces today is not far from the vision of the ideal classroom. Most companies are moving to become paperless, making their data entirely digital, with all information produced and received electronically. Emails are the norm as a means of communication, serving as an efficient productivity tool; and video conferencing and telecommuting replace the need for long commutes and expensive travel arrangements. Clearly, most organizations recognize how the incorporation of technology enhances productivity. The natural evolution of education, then, is to follow the example set by the workplace by providing highly advanced technological tools not only for learning but also for the development of learning through technological avenues. Technology integration in the classroom empowers students by engaging them with the very technological sources and tools that will ultimately prepare them for employment in their future workplaces.

Our technology-rich world is not limited to just the workplace. There is no question that this is an age saturated by digital media. The number of internet users has risen from 2.6 million in 1990 to 3 billion in 2014 (Murphy & Roser, 2016). Technologies such as tablets, cell phones, and video-game consoles are commonplace in most households in the United States. Computers have evolved to become faster, smaller, more visual, and more portable. From wearable technology like smartwatches to the "Internet of Things," including such technologies as smart appliances, society has become entrenched with immediate data and responsive feedback. Our cell phones tell us when we have to be somewhere via alarms and calendar apps, and then how to get there via GPS technology.

Adolescents and teenagers are using technology in more ways than ever before. They are growing up equipped with multimedia tools that significantly impact the world around them. Home telephones and standard postal mail have been replaced by the virtual world of cell phones, which are not only easily accessible but typically come with chat, text messaging, instant video conferencing, and email functions. Students no longer have to wait to go to the library to research a topic in the printed sources that are physically available there. The internet, with its many search engines and online libraries, makes data obtainable in an instant. Moreover, resources are not limited to those published by select sources. Knowledge can be accessed from people and sources all around the world. The time of waiting for the development of photographs and being unable to edit them is also gone. Today, students have the ability to make and edit their own photos and videos at little cost and with great ease. There are currently 1 billion YouTube users and 8 billion Facebook videos per day (source, date).

Consider the future with the proliferation of drones and 3D printing. Using their cell phones to navigate, children can fly drones above the trees and view the world from a new perspective. Printing actual 3D objects will become as commonplace as printing reports once was. That which we could not accomplish due to physical limitations in the past is becoming a reality in the present. Modern technology makes things that once took a great deal of time and advanced knowledge instantly available to most people.

Does technology have the ability to drive a student-centered pedagogy? Numerous studies offer evidence that teachers require sufficient technological competency in order to drive pedagogical change and achieve maximum student learning (Guzman & Nussbaum, 2009; Higgins, Beauchamp, & Miller, 2007). The goal of effective technology integration is to successfully embed technology use in education in order to drive a student-centered, investigative-based learning environment. Simply buying technology and urging teachers and students to use it does not meet this objective. To determine the actual benefits of integrating any technology as conventional classroom equipment, one of the crucial questions to answer is whether or not technological engagement actually does promote student-centered education.

Not all teachers teach the same way, and in that same regard, not every student learns the same way. When learners attribute a feeling of pride to a specific subject, they are more likely to become intrinsically motivated to master it. Motivation is often construed to be the stimulus that incites students to complete a task—the reward, either intrinsic or extrinsic in nature. Motivation is generally considered to be that influence that inspires and encourages students to engage in and complete activities that result in meaningful learning.

The inclusion of drones in instructional activities ultimately yields an increase in student motivation and engagement. The use of robotics in general allows students to have concrete examples of how STEM concepts are applied and utilized in the real world. A short exposure to robotics can have a lasting impact on students to pursue complex careers that they may have never considered. This is important, as it is projected that the nation will have up to 8 million STEM jobs by 2018 (Langdon, McKittrick, Beede, Khan, & Doms, 2011).

Outside of education, the use of drones is growing—particularly in the workplace, where applications are no longer limited to military or police operations. Scientists, construction workers, realtors, first responders, sports teams, band directors, and many more professionals are finding the utility of these quad copters, fueling a demand that this technology will quickly become a staple for college and career readiness.

In schools, drones are rapidly expanding in use and versatility as well. In science and engineering classes, students are building drones and writing the programs to steer them. School administrators are utilizing the technology to create marketing materials for YouTube channels and websites, showcasing their school and grounds from a bird's eye view. Sports programs enlist drones to record the action in the athletic fields below.

In the curriculum, drones present a possibility of a broad range of applications. Just to take a simple flight or to plan a route, students need to consider weight, height, angles, and speed. The key to the learning experience is to reinforce content knowledge with technology—in this case, drones. The drones grab the students' attention and engage them in an activity as they apply and master the skills that they learned during instruction.

Incidental Learning

A key element of teaching with the drone is the concept of incidental learning: students become so completely engaged by the use of the drone that they are not focused on the fact that they are applying concepts from the course content. Incidental learning is the unplanned learning that occurs during instructional activities and can occur in social situations (Kerka & Eric, 2000). It can arise as a byproduct of another event, such as "an experience, observation, reflection, interaction, unique event, or common routine task" (Konetes, 2011, p. 7). And incidental learning has a long tradition, with evidence dating back to decades when intentional and incidental learning could occur simultaneously during the same instructional activity (Cohen, 1967).

Children will spend countless hours in front of a screen, trying to accomplish missions in a video game that has no reward other than the value awarded to it by the player. As students, however, these same children may have difficulty finishing homework, paying attention in class, or finding a reason to be interested in a lesson. When students perceive the use of drones as an enjoyable activity—as an act of play as opposed to a learning activity—it can be a powerful motivator, impacting student enjoyment of the lesson (Carnahan, 2012). In other words, the problem is not always in the child; the instructor has to find a way to properly motivate the learner. The inclusion of drones as an application of concept is one way to do this, providing the hook that many students need to be engaged in the lesson and actively interested in learning.

Compared to most other technology, drones have the ability to gain and hold student attention in a unique way. Almost every student wants to fly a drone, and even if they are not actively controlling it, their attention is on it while it is in the air. While students make no differentiation between formal or incidental learning, the unintended outcomes of an incidental-learning experience often have a greater impact on the learner than the original lesson objectives (McFerrin, 1999).

Incidental learning is reported to show an improvement in self-confidence and self-determination, for instance (McFerrin, 1999). This aligns with the use of drones to get quiet and introverted students collaborating and communicating during group activities. Teachers have reported that students who never speak will take part in group work and even answer questions to the whole group when drones are included in the teaching method or lesson.

The inclusion of drones also allows teachers to differentiate the lesson and reach students who may not be not be interested in the subject matter. Putting the focus of activity on the drone while applying mathematics concepts during the flight times creates the perfect conditions for incidental learning. And gaining knowledge that is a product of incidental learning includes positive outcomes like a greater retention of information than that of the traditional lecture (Younes & Asay, 2003). The use of drones goes beyond simple instructional benefits and concept mastery because it impacts student engagement, communication, collaboration, and other important classroom components.

Teachers will enjoy the benefits of increased participation in the classroom and the real potential to impact the non-observable affective elements such as self-confidence. Anecdotal experience has shown that interactions with technologies such as drones and robotics can also have long-term effects on students who want to continue their interest in STEM-related fields. Children often desire more interaction with drones and robotics, and thereby evolve their use into more advanced skills. The use of drones and robotics may just be that spark that inspires certain students to change their life trajectory or career choices.

SOAR Model

Dr. Chris Carnahan and Dr. Laura Zieger, two of the authors of this book, have created a drone implementation model for educators looking to establish a drone program in a K–12 setting. The SOAR (safety, operation, active learning, and research) model is meant to provide a framework for educators looking to not only learn more about drones but ultimately implement them in an instructional setting. SOAR is focused on the user experience while providing research-based foundations for ethical, legal, and pragmatic utilization. Figure 1.1 outlines the SOAR model and its components.

Safety	Ethics and legal issues
Operation	Flight, maintenance, and troubleshooting
Active Learning	Engagement in solving problems
Research	Practical applications

Figure 1.1 The SOAR implementation model for drone usage in a K–12 educational setting

The SOAR model has been the basis of numerous successful district and school-level implementations. The approach takes the time to ensure that a holistic approach is taken to cover all the relevant aspects of the technology and its integration into schools. Too often in education, technology is funneled into classrooms without proper vetting and thorough evaluation of its effectiveness. Just because a technology is flashy does not necessarily mean that it will promote learning.

The use of drones engages, motivates, and inspires students to learn in ways that no other technology will allow. This alternative to traditional instruction easily grabs the students' attention, but safety must be a first priority. You must ensure the well-being of the operator, students, and institution. There are many considerations when operating the drones—especially outdoors—and uninformed operators present a potential liability to both the students and the school. It is crucial for users to be knowledgeable about all safety aspects to avoid potentially harmful situations.

Operation is concerned with the actual mechanics involved in flying and maintaining the drone. In the classroom, teachers may be without assistance, so they need to know how to safely fly the drone and how to quickly resolve minor issues. Comprehensive training on the classroom's drone will make the instructor feel comfortable using the device with students. Additionally, having a basic level of problem-solving skills for issues that occur with the drone (such as connecting the drone and controller, or inspecting and repairing a damaged blade—shown in Figure 1.2) will minimize any impact that these events have on instructional activities. With limited instructional time, it is especially important that teachers be proficient with their drone to ensure safety and maximize the educational impact.

Figure 1.2 Operators should be familiar and comfortable with inspecting a drone and replacing parts.

Active learning is another critical component of using drones in the classroom. The concept of active learning can be defined as "anything course related that all students in a class session are called upon to do other than simply watching, listening, and taking notes" (Felder & Brent, 2009). Classroom utilization features a technology that engages students and inspires them to energetically participate in lessons. Whether the drone is used to collect information, demonstrate concepts, or hook students' attention, it will be clear that students are immersed in the lesson.

Research is an often-overlooked component of technology deployment. Technology changes at such a rapid rate that traditional research generally lags behind adoption and implementation. And this can cause problems, as the technology cannot be thoroughly vetted and best practices cannot be developed. A haphazard approach to technology leads to misuses, unforeseen issues, and a loss of time and money. The best approach is to follow the recommendations of researchers and leaders in the field who have successfully implemented the technology. An efficient implementation maximizes the return on investment, so take a holistic approach that examines policy, professional development, and ultimately, effective classroom utilization.

Common Core State Standards

In 2015, students began taking the Algebra I PARCC (Partnership for Assessment of Readiness for College and Careers) assessment, which is aligned to the Common Core State Standards. New Jersey is the only state in the nation using the PARCC exams to make graduation determinations in 2016. Starting with the class of 2021, students may be required to pass the PARCC Algebra 1 exam in order to graduate. According to the New Jersey Department of Education (2013), "In the NJ School Performance Report, Algebra I course taking is highlighted as an indicator of college and career readiness because it remains one of the most significant early predictors that a student is capable of rigorous coursework, and is on track to graduate from high school and attend postsecondary education" (p. 8).

Startling recent test results have been a cause for alarm. In a recent report to the New York Board of Regents, three-quarters of New York's high school students flunked the Common Core algebra state standards–based test in 2014 (Campanile, 2015). New Jersey schools did not fare much better; less than half of the students scored as proficient at every level on the math tests, and only 2% of high school students who took the Algebra II test scored as proficient (NJ State Board of Education, 2015). As a result, students in middle school are being introduced to algebraic equations and concepts earlier in order to prepare them for the more complex Common Core State Standards–based Algebra I. (The CCSS integrate algebraic concepts in earlier grades, making CCSS middle school math curriculum more challenging than the traditional curriculum.)

The New Jersey Department of Education is motivating middle schools to offer Algebra I as one of its college-and-career-readiness benchmarks. The current target is for 20% of all students in school to take Algebra I in eighth grade (Erlichson, 2015). As far back as 1997, the U.S. Department of Education found that students who take algebra in high school attend college at a much higher rate, with low-income students being three times more likely to go to college (U.S. Department of Education, 1997). Other studies further indicate that "[students who] successfully complete Algebra I often continue to pursue the study of high school mathematics that prepares them for college, while students who are unsuccessful in Algebra I find their path to success blocked" (University of Nebraska-Lincoln, n.d., p. 1). According to RAND and Ball (2003), "Without proficiency in algebra, students cannot access a full range of educational and career options, and they have limited chances of success" (p. 47).

One concern is that these middle school students will not be able to comprehend the subject at an earlier age. While there is research showing that students who take Algebra I in eighth grade are more likely to successfully attend college, the National Council of Teachers of Mathematics warns that pushing students to take it before they are ready often leads to failure (Gojak, 2013).

Historically, middle school math was overhauled in the 1990s, when the concern was that the United States was lagging behind other developed countries. Algebra became a national goal. Eventually, concerns began to surface regarding teachers' ability to teach the subject, leaving students underprepared. The Brown Center at Brookings Institution report "The Misplaced Math Student: Lost in Eighth Grade Algebra" illustrated that having more students take algebra did not necessarily mean they were learning. High-income students were getting private tutoring to help them along while lower-income students (with less means for private instruction) were failing (Loveless, 2008).

Achievement in STEM subjects is a ladder toward promoting equity for all ethnic groups and socioeconomic statuses by providing access to academic and career success. Further, it has become a gatekeeper for the less advantaged to access high-status and income-producing occupations. Hundreds of thousands of students across the country are ending their education without having the mathematical and science skills they need to be educated citizens and consumers.

Algebra is an essential subject to developing students' ability to learn how to reason with facts; it is the building block for higher-level mathematics. Many of the concepts presented in Algebra I are progressions of the concepts that were introduced in Grades 6 through 8. According to the 2010 draft proposed for the New Jersey Algebra I Core Content, the mission is "[for] students to use mathematics to make sense of the world around them. They use mathematical reasoning to pose and solve problems, communicating their solutions and solution strategies through a variety of representations" (p. 1). The proposal further states, "Students studying Algebra I should use appropriate tools (e.g., algebra tiles to explore operations with polynomials, including factoring) and technology, such as regular opportunities to use graphing calculators and spreadsheets. Technological tools assist in illustrating the connections between algebra and other areas of mathematics, and demonstrate the power of algebra" (p. 1).

The Common Core emphasizes conceptual understanding at every phase of math instruction, including algebraic concepts. How can these abstract ideas and concepts be taught to students at the middle school level? Students in middle school should be drawing bar graphs based on experiences, conducting experiments, discovering and generating patterns, and following and writing directions for carrying out tasks. These students can then build their understanding of statistics, probability, and discrete mathematics based on these previous activities.

American K–12 students still fall behind other industrialized countries. According to a recent PEW report, at the age of 15, United States students ranked 35th out of 64 countries in mathematics (DeSilver, 2015). Unfortunately, the more abstract math becomes, the less students are interested. This is particularly pertinent during the middle school years, when teachers often have fewer options to explain abstract concepts. But technology such as drones, or UAVs, can help students understand the significance of a quadratic equation.

By using UAVs, abstract math is brought to life through the power of visual and hands-on learning.

Essential Questions

Essential conceptual questions that can be addressed by utilizing drones in the curriculum include:

- What are some ways to represent, describe, and analyze patterns that occur in our world?

- When is one representation of a function more useful than another?

- How can we use algebraic representation to analyze patterns?

- Why is it useful to represent real-life situations algebraically?

- How can change be best represented mathematically?

- How can we use mathematical language to describe change?

- How can we use mathematical models to describe change or change over time?

- How can patterns, relations, and functions be used as tools to best describe and help explain real-life situations?

- How can the collection, organization, interpretation, and display of data be used to answer questions?

- How can the representation of data influence decisions?

- When does order matter?

- How can experimental and theoretical probabilities be used to make predictions or to draw conclusions?

The United States National Education Technology Plan (NETP) supports the implementation of STEM-related teaching, indicating that technology should be used to support student interaction with STEM content in ways that promote understanding of complex concepts, engage complex problem solving, generate opportunities for STEM learning, and prepare for the future workplace. According to Dr. Chris Dede, the Timothy E. Wirth Professor in Learning Technology at Harvard Graduate School of Education, "Many, if not most, teachers in STEM fields will be hard pressed to get from industrial-style instruction to deeper learning without the vehicles of digital tools, media, and experiences" (2015).

ISTE Standards for Teachers

As a result of the changing times, technology literacy has become a required skill for education professionals and their students to successfully participate in the current global economy. The International Society for Technology Education (ISTE) created the ISTE Standards for Teachers to align with their vision of what a technology-enriched learning environment should include. The standards promote the idea that teachers should incorporate diverse technologies in their teaching in order to best address students' needs and provide creative lessons that engage learners.

According to ISTE, educators need new expertise and pedagogical understanding to "teach, work, and learn in the digital age" (source). The ISTE standards consist of five benchmarks for teachers: (1) student learning and creativity, (2) digital-age learning experiences and assessments, (3) digital-age work and learning, (4) digital citizenship and responsibility, and (5) teachers' professional growth and leadership. The general focus of the standards is to cultivate the best possible conditions for success. Though teachers are expected to create a certain learning environment for their students, they are also compelled to model the example of lifelong learning themselves.

Keeping current with emerging technologies demonstrates to students that education is a never-ending journey. With robotics and drones becoming so prolific in society, the knowledge and skills required to operate and program UAVs is a necessary technological literacy.

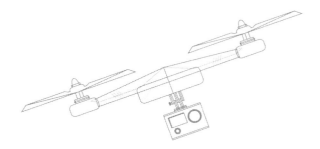

CHAPTER 2

Introducing Drones in the Classroom

Teaching can be a challenging profession—one that requires adaption to an ever-changing environment. Curricula are revised constantly, and programs can come and go in the blink of an eye. The pressure of expectations for high test scores, diminishing school budgets, and copious amounts of paperwork can leave teachers feeling stressed and emotionally exhausted. In addition, teachers must find a way to prepare students for the digital age with a set of skills that they can transfer into college and the workforce.

With all of their obligations, it is understandable why teachers may not be overly enthusiastic about a new initiative. Many seasoned teachers have experienced fads in education and do not want to waste their time with "the next best thing." However, all teachers share the desire to make a significant, lasting contribution to their students' lives.

This chapter contains the stories of two teachers who made the decision to implement drones in their lessons. Though their teaching backgrounds are different, their goal is the same: to implement engaging and effective lessons in order to prepare their students for future success.

Two Teachers' Stories

Wayne Creed, General-Education Teacher

Wayne Creed is an elementary school teacher of fourteen years in an urban, public school district. He currently teaches a fifth grade inclusion class. An inclusion class consists of general-education students, and special-education students. He teaches all subjects: mathematics, language arts, science, and social studies. Wayne has received the Teacher of the Year district recognition twice since becoming a teacher.

Wayne believes the biggest challenges in education right now are student comprehension of all the information necessary for skill mastery and keeping students engaged in these rigorous lessons. He believes there are some key reasons for the existing achievement gap: learning disabilities, the amount of assistance a student receives at home, and a lack of student engagement in instructional material and topics. Information retention is impossible when student engagement is minimal; conversely, information retention increases when students are curious and interested.

Wayne is the mathematics representative for his school and attends monthly mathematics meetings in his district. During a break at a meeting, his supervisor approached him to propose an idea. She was short and to the point.

Deloitte.

Suzann by b

Budget

Eoin McGread

eoinmcgread@hotmail.com

C 7 9 7 9 3 5 5 3
6 5

Kiera

Tay Problem

Radu Bak

23rd Jan

BAKING | RSA

2 came pent

Future/by bn

"We are doing something different," she told him. "Before you react, I want you to take some time to think about it."

Wayne's interest was piqued (he has a reputation for being a creative and engaging teacher).

She continued, "We are getting drones and using them during mathematics instruction—not as a gimmick or a toy but as a learning tool. I will not say too much now; only that I'm very excited about it, and it is going to change education forever. Yes, I know that is a bold statement, but it is true. I want you to be a part of it."

That is all that she told him as the break ended and the meeting continued.

During Wayne's interview for this book he was asked about his initial thoughts when he was first approached with the idea of using drones in the classroom during mathematics instruction.

He recalls, "My initial thought when she first told me about this was, 'What the heck? What is she doing?'"

Once he went back to his seat, he reflected on the drone concept, and the idea became much more interesting to him. He realized how exciting and fun it would be for the students. Within 10 minutes, he was up again to talk to his supervisor. He provided three ideas on how to incorporate drones into a math lesson, and he stated then and there that he wanted to be a part of the drone initiative—part of a change in how he educated his students.

He returned to his table and began speaking about it with the other teachers. The professional-development provider was not happy with all the distraction, but the excitement could not be contained. At the completion of that workshop, everyone was intrigued with the notion of incorporating technology into the classroom via drones.

Two months went by with no official word on when Wayne would be getting a drone to use during mathematics instruction. That did not hinder Wayne's ambition, however. He continued developing ways to integrate drones into lessons; and when the announcement was made that his public school division was implementing a drone initiative, he was ready.

Wayne attended an informational session for the new drone initiative. He observed the looks on other teachers' faces as they heard about drones and their proposed usage for the first time. The looks of astonishment were identical to the first time he heard about the concept. Having already considered the various capabilities, Wayne actively participated during the informational session, sharing ideas on how these drones could be integrated into mathematics instruction.

Wayne was one of twenty-two teachers selected for the drone initiative. The district provided him with three professional-development sessions on implementing drones into the existing mathematics curriculum. The training consisted of lessons on safety, ethics, and legality of use using the SOAR model. Additionally, teachers were trained on the operations aspects of drones: flight maintenance and troubleshooting. The teachers worked collaboratively to develop lesson plans and strategies for implementing the drones into the mathematics curriculum. During the workshop, time was also allotted for instructional demonstrations. Participants were shown how to edit drone footage using free movie-editing software. During this time, teachers from schools all over the district—many of whom had never met before—developed into a true professional-learning community. They shared tips and tricks and advice on how to overcome challenges. Collaborating in much the same way that their lessons asked of their students, teachers developed exciting activities to teach difficult subjects with the help of drones.

Wayne credits the professional development he received as a factor in the success he has had with the drone initiative. He feels that learning how to set up and fly a drone, as well as learning ways to implement it in the classroom, made him more confident and comfortable. Being able to collaborate with other teachers in the district was also an invaluable asset.

Wayne describes the students' reactions when he told them they would be using drones during math as being much different than his initial reaction: "Their initial reaction was what mine eventually came to be, which was excitement and fun. They were blown away that they were going to have an opportunity to fly drones and actually use them to demonstrate math concepts."

According to Wayne, it was not challenging to teach the students to operate the drones. It took 45 minutes for every student to fly the drone and become proficient at safe flight operations. Wayne began by giving his students a full lesson on the safety, rules, and operational procedures for drones—the first step in the SOAR model. In order for students to operate the drone, they had to pass a safety quiz he created. In addition, all students had to bring in photo-release forms signed by a parent, allowing them to be videoed by the drone.

Students were assigned to two groups, with each group receiving a drone. Wayne made the decision to let the students use iPads to control their drone, rather than cell phones. He modeled how to take off and land; how to fly forward, backward, and side-to-side; and how to turn the drone around. Then he and an assisting teacher, each working with a group, had every student fly the drone a certain distance forward, turn it around, and fly it back. This was all it took for students to feel comfortable. A few students were a bit nervous at first, but that hesitation quickly disappeared after they took their turns.

Wayne is fortunate to be working in a building with extremely supportive administrators who believe in the benefits of implementing technology in education. His principal is always looking for ways to enhance student engagement. The administrators observed the class learning to fly the drone and Wayne's introductory lesson. They also observed the increase in student engagement. As a result, the principal and assistant principal immediately decided that a drone program in their building was paramount to increasing student engagement in all appropriate classes. That same day, the administrators ordered seven additional drones. Since then, they have expanded their fleet of drones to include land drones and professional drones, and they even have a drone cabinet for storage. Among the fleet is a Parrot AR.Drone 2.0, a DJI Phantom 3 Professional, a Parrot Bebop, and a Parrot Jumping Sumo minidrone.

Wayne's biggest challenge thus far is keeping up with the maintenance of the drones. Batteries have to be charged frequently, and propellers have to be checked for chips. Another challenge has been securing physical space for the lessons. Since his building has many drones, each group gets its own during a lesson. Space is needed to fly multiple drones simultaneously. Either the gym or the auditorium has to be reserved or, weather permitting, the class moves outside of the building. Drones can operate in the classroom environment, but now that students are used to having one drone per group, Wayne plans accordingly.

Wayne has done a variety of math lessons incorporating the drones, including dividing decimals, estimation, and conversions. After each lesson, he reflects on what worked, what did not, and what could be improved for next time. The first lesson started with one drone and now lessons incorporate up to four drones. That means the students fly the drones at the same time, which keeps them fully engaged; there is no idle time.

It is rare to observe a math lesson where Wayne is actually flying a drone. The class works independently, and Wayne serves as the facilitator of learning. His most recent instructional evaluation exemplifies this point: "The students took the initiative to adapt the lesson to make it relevant. Students were engaged in higher-order thinking and class discussion. They assisted each other in under-standing the content and took initiative in improving their work."

Wayne feels like the drone initiative has had a positive impact on his instruction too. It forces him to be more creative in the way he presents a particular standard. He "thinks outside the box" to teach a concept creatively as opposed to conducting a lesson in front of an interactive whiteboard. A creative teacher is beneficial to a class since he or she affords students various adaptations to a variety of learning styles.

Additionally, Wayne believes students will now have a much better reference of prior knowledge when they take a standardized test. He gives an example of a lesson they did on units and measurements using drones: "If they have a question like this on a standardized test, they will have a recall memory to tie it to. They will think, 'We converted inches into feet [and] into yards when we were flying the drone. I remember how to do that.'"

If you ask a student if they remember practicing a specific skill in a lesson, many times they cannot. Wayne thinks by utilizing drones, students will recall, "Yes, that was December when we went into the gym with the drones."

Wayne does not see drone integration in education as a fad. He feels that the more the other classes see his students using the drones, the more they will want to be involved. His building also provided professional development on drone integration, in addition to the professional development provided by his district. As he disseminates that training and information to other staff members, he hopes drone integration will become more widespread throughout the school.

Wayne fully supports the use of drones in mathematics and has agreed to participate in a research study regarding implementation. Students will be given a pretest and posttest with drone lessons serving as a teaching tool. He thinks it will be a great way to measure success and plans to eventually expand the use of drones into other content areas. For now, however, he wants to concentrate on getting more comfortable with creating lessons for math and its standards. Then, once the drones have been successfully aligned to the Common Core State Standards for mathematics, he will move on to other subjects. He already has several ideas for interdisciplinary projects.

Upon reflection, Wayne recalls the initial reaction of the other teachers: "How will we use drones for math?" He laughs about it now because the ideas come effortlessly; in fact, his students have even developed their own ideas for implementation.

Claire Seborowski, *Primary Autism Teacher*

Claire Seborowski teaches a K–2 autism class in an urban, public school district. Before taking over this role, she was a first grade inclusion teacher. Claire's student population consists of three students who are advanced academically but deficient socially, and three students who are deficient academically but advanced socially.

When Claire talks about challenges in education, she naturally references the population that she teaches. But she recognizes that she is in a fortunate situation. Her school is a K–2 building with a large special-needs population. Her administrator is a true instructional leader who believes every student can achieve, and ensures that all students are included and recognized. Claire knows that every building is not like this; she has heard stories, read articles, and seen news segments that are contrary to her situation.

Claire feels that the biggest problem with primary autism classes is that they are not integrated with the general-education classrooms as much as they should be. Some teachers who are not in the primary autism setting may wonder what these students really have to offer. However, if teachers gave autistic students a chance to participate, she knows the teachers would see that they could improve the dynamic of a general-education classroom. She describes the intelligence of her students as "through the roof."

Claire believes students' difficulty with problem solving is directly related to an inability to apply knowledge. Like most teachers (regardless of the subject area, grade level, or population they teach), she feels that students struggle to understand how skills learned in the classroom environment connect to solutions of problems outside of school. The students have recall ability, but when it comes time for application, they cannot. She knows that making the material meaningful by providing her students with opportunities for real-world connection is vital to their success.

When Claire first heard her school was selected to begin implementing drones in the classroom, she was apprehensive. Her principal explained that the school was part of an initiative to use drones in classroom instruction and told Claire not to worry; she had spoken at length with the administrator running the initiative, and they believed it would provide a great opportunity for the students.

Claire had no idea how drone integration would work. She knew nothing about drones, aside from negative news stories regarding them being flown into commercial airspace and the paparazzi using them for celebrity pictures. She was especially concerned about how drones could be applied to her population of students; however, she trusted her principal and the administrator running the initiative. Claire was confident they would never put her or her students in a compromising situation, so she decided to accept the proposed idea. Today, Clare is grateful she made this decision, as the results have been astounding.

To begin the process, Claire attended a meeting outlining the drone initiative. The purpose of the initiative was to increase student engagement by implementing drones during core subject lessons. The informational meeting also established the requirements to participate. Although there were several, two resonated with Claire: (1) The drone had to be implemented for instructional purposes. "How will my class use this during math?" she wondered. And (2) students were to control the drone. Teachers were expected to model the lesson, but flying and demonstrating proficiency were the responsibility of the student. Teachers were told this was mandatory—the drone was a learning tool, not a toy. As she had never flown a drone before, Claire herself was worried about her own abilities to do so. Could her students do it?

Claire's apprehension started to ease after the first professional-development session. She learned that drones were actually safe and difficult to break. Learning about drone safety made her feel comfortable using a drone with her students, and seeing the foam guard around the drone made her less concerned with injuries. After several hours of practice, lesson planning, and developing real-world activities, Claire's confidence increased.

She returned from the professional development determined to successfully integrate drones into her classroom instruction; she saw it as an exciting way to showcase her students' unique abilities. Having worked with students with autism most of her career, she knew that implementing drones in her classroom would likely require a different approach than other teachers use. She knew that given the broad spectrum of abilities within her class, she would have to customize the lessons to meet the individual needs of her students.

Claire's students were excited during the initial drone demonstration. Claire and another teacher brought their primary autism classes to the auditorium, where Claire placed the drone on the stage floor. She began by explaining a brief history of drones and then proceeded to fly the drone around the open space of the auditorium. The students were amazed. Some students watched while others covered their eyes and ears. One student compared it to a flying saucer while another exclaimed, "I can feel the wind!" Claire was pleased with the instant engagement and reaction it sparked.

In alignment with the SOAR model, Claire went over drone safety and the importance of giving adequate space when a fellow classmate is controlling the drone. Then she and her colleague began to try to get the lower-functioning students to focus on the drone. Many of those students do not make eye contact and/or do not observe during instructional activities, so they cover their faces. (Claire has since found that, over time, this has changed. Now when the drone flies by, these students lift their heads and are fixated. Incredibly, they watch and focus on the drone's flight, even if it is only briefly.)

During the drone introduction lesson, each student used the controller to fly the drone. They first started practicing with takeoff and landing. Claire admits that it was challenging to teach her class to fly the drone, but she emphasizes that it takes her students more time to attain most skills. The difference with the drone is that her students were eager to learn, and this willingness motivated them to practice until they achieved proficiency. Despite many crashes into the floor and walls, no injuries occurred. As a result, most students exhibited confidence when flying. After several days of practice, the students demonstrated more competence in their flights, flying the drone in all directions, as well as turning the drone around.

As soon as Claire and her colleague were assured their students were no longer afraid of the drone, they invited some second grade general-education students to the auditorium to observe their autism classes using the drones with distinct aptitude. The connection was made, and the primary autism students assisted the second graders with flying the drone. All students involved were engaged in meaningful social interactions, and everyone was included regardless of classification. Claire says creating inclusive environments is common in her building, but the conversations, teamwork, and lasting connections the drones created was something she had never observed before. These activities not only reinforced core subject skills, they also developed socialization skills, which are distinctly difficult for students with autism.

Claire recalls walking in the hallway with her class when a student pointed out a second grader: "Ms. Seborowski! He is helping our group with the drones during math." The drone initiative is helping her students create friendships. She also acknowledges that encouraging verbal communication from her students is a difficult task, but the drone activities have definitely helped: "The other day, a girl in my class said, 'This is amazing.' She never uses words like that."

Claire's students ask about the drone all the time; they want to know when they will be flying it again, and they want to know why they are not using it during reading and writing too. These simple inquiries have made Claire realize that the drone can be integrated during reading and writing instruction, so she has begun to draft lesson plans that involve taking pictures with the drone and using the images to make predictions.

Using the drone, Claire makes lessons fun and exciting. Her class is currently learning to count by twos. She puts numbers on the floor, and the students count aloud ("Two, four, six…") as a student flies the drone from one number to the next in the series. The drone integration helps with math but also develops students' fine-motor skills. In addition, students are making the connection that drones are for education. When students return to their classes after a lesson with the drone, they articulate that they were working with solid figures or skip counting using the drone; they do not describe using the drone as playing.

Parents have told Claire that their children have come home talking about the drone and how they've been using it during mathematics instruction. The parents are happy because this has enhanced the conversation and social interaction at home. Their children are excited about learning and cannot wait to talk about flying the drone to solid figures, like a cube. Then they proceed to describe the geometric traits of the cube.

All students in Claire's building are excited about the drone, and students in different classes are requesting to assist with drone lessons. Claire wishes she could have every student in the auditorium at once but knows that is impossible. She is trying to create a schedule that will eventually allow every student to have an opportunity to assist with a drone lesson. With additional professional development, she hopes that more teachers will be part of her school district's drone initiative.

Claire feels that using the drone during instruction has changed her perspective as a teacher. "This has taught me a lot about teaching," she says. "For instance, with that one child that doesn't like to look up, that doesn't like to focus on anything. When I saw that, the fact that he looked up for even two seconds and smiled… was a major thing. It gave me many more ideas [about what] we could do with the special-ed population [to include] them with the general-ed population. It has opened my eyes to more activities that can take place."

Claire's ability to "think outside the box" has been enhanced. She thinks drones are the future of education and is excited about it—and her students notice that excitement and energy. She plans on using the drone during summer school, even exposing the pre-K, disabled classes to it.

Claire believes that drones are a current and relevant integration of technology for all students but especially for students with autism. The initiative has created a true example of inclusion, allowing her students to work with their general-education peers. It has helped her students develop social, language, and math skills. Claire credits using the drone during lessons with encouraging conversation from her students; with drawing out words and even sentences that her students would not normally say. The drone has allowed her students to engage in critical-thinking activities that demonstrate their learning and understanding through interactive technology.

Claire's advice to anyone who is considering implementing drone usage in their class or in their building: "Go for it!" It will provide a new outlook on teaching, and the direct result will be increased student engagement.

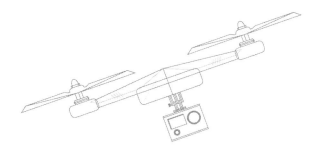

CHAPTER 3

Safety, Legal, and Ethical Issues

There is no denying the potential for learning and motivation that drones bring to an educational setting. However, as with any technology, there are rules that need to be followed in order to ensure the safety of students and avoid any legal issues. The key to success in the school setting is to know these rules and implement a common-sense approach through policies and practices that are institution-wide. It is critical that administrators and educators make this a priority.

Indoor Use

The outdoor flight of drones falls under the control and supervision of the Federal Aviation Administration (FAA). However, the indoor use of drones does not fall under the jurisdiction of the FAA. This means that drones used inside a building do not have to be registered or follow the guidelines and regulations for outdoor flight that are outlined in this chapter. The UAS (Unmanned Aircraft Systems) Q&A page on the FAA website provides more information on these guidelines (https://www.faa.gov/uas/registration/faqs/). You'll learn that the FAA is only concerned with navigable airspace and potential threats that would occur in this area.

The indoor use of drones does present its own challenges, as there are obviously more potential obstacles for the drone to encounter (walls, doors, ventilation systems, people, desks, and any other barrier that it can find). Depending on the size and construction of the device, teachers can use the drones inside the classroom, halls, and gyms. Indoor flight is more controlled in a confined space, where the drone cannot escape. The only issue that teachers should be aware of is the proximity to students or other humans. Indoor use alleviates federal regulations for the institution and instructor but does not discharge the concern of liability.

When using the drone inside, the focus should be on the activity and the design of the drone. Ensure that drones have bumpers or protectors that stop the propellers from striking objects and people. This will prevent harm to students and to the device itself. Indoor flight is a good solution for educators who still want to have students experience the motivational and educational benefits of drones without dealing with extraneous regulations or issues. Using drones indoors allows a multitude of uses but limits the focus to distance, height, and videography.

FAA Regulations

Drones are an evolving technology that has seen an enormous growth in popularity. As with any technology that experiences an explosion in usage, regulators have to rush to catch up. For most educators, using a piece of technology that falls under FAA control is something that they have probably never considered. For amateur aviators who have flown model helicopters for years, however, this is nothing new.

It is important to remember that UAVs and the policies that affect their operation are still in their infancy, so practices and legalities are likely to change in the future. Educators and users should be aware of these changes and understand that the legal considerations covered in this book may have already changed. It is always best to check the FAA website for current guidelines (FAA.gov). For now, the FAA has set up an initial series of guidelines that constitute what they consider safe and legal use of drones at this time.

There are several types of forbidden airspace that operators must avoid. First, users are required to stay below 400 feet. The vertical height that a drone is permitted to fly helps operators avoid what is considered navigable airspace. The FAA considers anything more than 500 feet as open airspace, where planes and helicopters operate. It is critical that UAV operators stay clear of manned aircraft. There have already been a number of incidents where drones have come into close contact with helicopters and airplanes, presenting a host of dangerous scenarios. Drones could potentially damage or disable engines or rotors on aircraft causing the manned aircraft to crash.

There are other restrictions to flight, including certain places where use is not allowed at all. For example, flying is not allowed within five miles of an airport unless the operator contacts and obtains permission from the tower. Another place to avoid is large, occupied stadiums. Stadiums that have a capacity of 30,000 seats or more are prohibited airspace for a distance of three miles around the event. Some states or local governments may have enacted other laws that govern how close operators may be to groups of people, even at high school sporting events.

Drones must stay under the control of the operator and not be used in a reckless or careless manner. This means that in addition to other aircraft, users need to avoid other humans as well. Although this comes from the FAA guidelines, it is just common sense and good practice to ensure that others are not at risk from being struck by the drone.

At this point, some readers may be thinking, "What am I getting myself into here, and how do I know how close an airport is located?" The good thing is that there is an app for locating no-fly zones. The B4UFLY app from the FAA uses your smartphone to do the research for you. This app is available in both Android and iOS platforms. Additionally, some more-advanced drones have a built-in application using their integrated GPS. For example, the DJI Phantom will not take off in Washington, DC, when in GPS mode. If you are experiencing an issue where the drone won't fly and you have a model with this capability, this may also be something worth looking into when troubleshooting.

Another important consideration when buying and using a drone is its weight. The weight of the drone is important in two regards. First, UAVs cannot exceed 55 pounds in total weight. This isn't an issue for most commercially viable models, but if you were working at an institution that had a drone club that was building from one from scratch, it is an important consideration. Second, if the drone weighs more than half a pound, it needs to be registered with the FAA. The online registration (https://www.faa.gov/uas/registration/) costs $5 and is valid for three years. Once the registration is processed, the owner must put a number on the drone. This can be done in the battery compartment as long as access to the compartment does not require any tools. Registering the drone allows officials to trace the owner of a drone flying illegally.

When flying the devices, operators must maintain a visual line of sight on their drone at all times. This means that you have to be able to physically see the drone with your eyes rather than on a screen. A popular modification or addition to drones has been using virtual-reality goggles, such as the Oculus Rift. However, this is a safety concern, as flying by video may limit the field of vision for the user. The drone camera may not pick up wires, trees, and other obstacles—especially with moving left, right, and backwards—so flying by line of sight is still the optimal method.

A major consideration of drone usage is the category under which it falls. Open use is limited to individuals who are using the drones for recreational, hobby, and educational purposes. But commercial usage has its own limits, as the FAA has strict oversight that requires these types of users to obtain special permission. This is the reason why you do not see reporters on the nightly news flying drones around news scenes. This aspect of the law is currently evolving, and operators should ensure that their use aligns to the current legal interpretations.

It is important to note that these guidelines represent the FAA's early operating and safety guidelines for drone operators. Drones are a relatively new technology, so the legislation is continually changing around them. It appears in some instances that there is a relaxing of the laws—as in the case of commercial usage where some companies are being given exemptions to fly drones when they were previously were denied—while on the other hand, more places are becoming restricted airspaces. Uses that do not align with the exempted cases can apply for an exemption through the FAA. The FAA's FAQ page for the Section 333 Petition for Exemption offers more information on this and other exemption concerns (www.faa.gov/uas/legislative_programs/section_333/333_faqs/).

In addition to the FAA oversight, it is important to know that some local municipalities have created their own ordnances that must be obeyed. For example, Los Angles requires that drone users register their devices with the city and fly a minimum of 25 feet away from people (Queally, 2016). Chicago prohibits the flying of drones over churches, schools, hospitals, and private property without permission (National Public Radio, 2015). These are just a few examples of why you must stay up to date on drone legislation, as the FAA is not the only organization that has asserted oversight on the usage of drones.

Avoid adverse legal situations by ensuring that all operators adhere to all legalities. Educators and administrators should consult with school attorneys in regard to operating a drone at their institution—to be certain that there are no unknown liabilities. Then follow the current regulations to the letter while keeping in mind that the legal status and oversight of drones is continually evolving as this technology emerges and grows. The content covered in this section may change depending on legislation—all the more reason to get the school attorneys on board.

Athletics

Drones provide an interesting perspective when filming high school sporting events. They can capture media and show the movement of athletes in a unique way that would otherwise be unfeasible or cost prohibitive. Numerous sports, and band groups are using the drones to record video. As a result, organizations and institutions have begun to review the use of drones during sporting events based on their competitive advantage and safety issues. For example, the North Carolina High School Athletics Association has instituted a ban on drones during all high school sporting events (Cook, 2015). Even some large districts such as the Broward County Athletic Association in Florida have instituted prohibitions on the use of drones during athletic events (Brousseu, 2015).

The issue of use in some of these cases may be due to the operation of drones by individuals who are not associated with the institution itself. Instead of limiting the use of drones to select individuals, organizations should implement specific policies to address their needs. And as research and knowledge about the safety and benefits of drones emerges, policy is likely to change.

Privacy and Image Usage

Owners of properties can still regulate the use of their land, and this includes the airspace. If flying a drone off of school property and on private property, it is important to ensure that there is permission to be there. Operators of drones need to respect private property laws—especially because privately owned property presents an interesting and unvetted legal issue. The often-used example is that of an unsolicited photo of a child: if a child is photographed in a fenced yard, the image is private; if the child's image is photographed in a park, then it is public. The case changes when a drone can go up 400 feet and make a six-foot fence meaningless. This creates unchartered territory as to what is considered private viewing versus public viewing.

The best rule of thumb when taking pictures or recording video that will be used or made public in one format or another is to ask permission and get media releases. Ensuring that permission is obtained for the location and the people there will eliminate any potential issues that could emerge. Most institutions have media-release policies, so it is best to adhere to them. Permission is essential when working with children, especially if images focus on one or two children in particular. Generally, in regard to public places, groups of people or children do not require permission to use the image if the individuals cannot be identified.

Local municipalities and organizations can also have their own laws and rules on photography, including aerial photography and privacy, so do your homework. An example of this would be the Florida Freedom from Unwarranted Surveillance Act (FUSA), which requires drone users to obtain permission to capture images of private property or people on private property (O'Connor, 2015).

Institutional Policies

The development of polices that address drone usage within an organization are critical for both teachers and administrators. Organizations should examine if drones can be incorporated into their acceptable use policies (AUPs) or if there is a need to create an independent policy that addresses this specific technology. Because the legal implications—both civil and criminal—are of serious consequences, organizations need to ensure that all bases are covered.

For educators, it is important to ensure that the organization has implemented a policy before students are involved. When there is a policy in place and it is being followed, it affords a level of protection because usage falls within acceptable practices. As drones can be controversial and even present a potential safety issue, having administrative support and protections enables usage without the fear of potential penalties. That way, if there is an unfortunate incident where damage or injury occurs, the outcome will be less critical to the students and the school alike.

Policies should include reference to FAA guidelines and what is considered acceptable usage for drones within the organization's scope. This includes what users can and cannot use the drone for, where it is permissible to fly the drone, and who may operate the technology. Will the teacher be the only one permitted to fly the drone outside of the building? Hopefully not, but this is one of the questions that needs to be covered within a policy.

Appendix A has an example of a drone policy that has been written and implemented within a higher-education institution. The contents were created after examining other organizational policies, discussion with administrators, and involvement of legal counsel. This example may not work in every organization but can serve as a good place to start with discussions within a district. As the legal environment surrounding drones continues to evolve, it is important that policy is reviewed and updated on a continual basis. Organizations should consult with their legal counsel on all new policies.

Subsequently, institutions should develop their own policies in regard to external use of drones on school grounds. This should limit outside use when it's considered trespassing and is prosecuted as such. This will also ensure that the use of drones is restricted to trained school personnel, protecting the privacy of students and the well-being of all persons on the school campus.

Liability

One of the biggest concerns surrounding the use of drones is the potential liability that their use can present. Educators should be aware that there is a risk of injury, damage to the drone or other property, and even civil penalties. The key to successful implementation is to be aware of potential risks and practice safe operations. It is no different than the use of chemicals in a science lab, where preparedness and safety procedures are developed and adhered to in order to avoid negative situations.

Institutions should consult with their legal counsel prior to implementing a drone program to ensure that policies and practice align to relevant laws. Administrators should also review insurance coverage so that the use of drones is covered by the institution's policy in regard to liability.

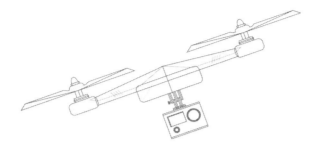

CHAPTER 4

Selection and Operation of a Drone

P rior to purchasing a drone, as with any technology, consideration needs to be given to what drone implementation is supposed to accomplish. Identifying the need, audience, and purpose should guide the selection of the drone. Too often, technology is purchased without thinking through the process of how end users will apply it. Will the drone be used to increase student engagement, motivation, or achievement? These devices have the ability to do all three but only if there is a cohesive process to select drones, train users, and support implementation.

Applications

The drone selection process should primarily be driven by doing a needs analysis and using this process to guide choices. This means that the intended utilization in the classroom should drive the purchasing process. This bottom-up approach ensures that money is well spent and that the needs of the teachers and students are the focus of the technology purchase. A drone that is going to be used to produce media elements at the high school level is going to have different requirements than one that is simply going to be used for estimation of height at the elementary level. A drone should meet the needs of the intended user and its educational purposes to optimize the investment on technology.

The remainder of this chapter will focus on the major considerations in purchasing a drone, but the basis for decisions should remain centered on the objective of the implementation. Ultimately, the goal (as with any technology) is to ensure that the drone is used in a manner that increases student achievement, engagement, and motivation. Thinking about what the drone will do during a lesson is the key component in choosing the correct model to accomplish the goal. A good rule is to go for a slightly higher model, because once a drone is purchased, there will be uses and applications realized that were not even considered. Drones have the ability to expand the motivation of not just students but teachers to explore creative applications.

Cost

Today, there are a wide variety of drones in all price ranges from minidrones (that can cost $25) to quasi-professional models (that cost more than $4,000). Trying to identify which model is best should not necessarily be based just on cost. Again, this should be aligned to district, school, or classroom objectives. In Chapter 7, we will highlight some of the ways to receive external support to fund the purchase of these devices, but for the classroom teacher trying to gain administrative support, it is important to show the utility that drones will bring to the classroom. Administrators often support the purchase of equipment that brings prominence and innovation to the classroom and to the school, especially if it advances instructional activities. This means to justify the cost, a clear proposal should be created to illustrate the benefits of the technology and to show how other schools are implementing it. Walk through a school with a drone (or even just the drone box) and watch every child—and adult—look at it and comment about it. There is an undeniable hook with these devices.

The cost is generally relative to the technology and imaging ability that are built into each platform. Additionally, sensors, GPS systems, and controllers impact the cost of the product. Although the costs are continually dropping as the technology becomes more mainstream, there is still a considerable cost for some models. Initial purchase price is a consideration and a gatekeeper for some institutions, but it should not be the only factor. Any technology that does not meet the needs of the classroom teacher will be doomed to the storage cabinet and result in zero impact on the investment. The goal is to balance cost and classroom effectiveness.

The typical cost of a drone for classroom use can be anywhere between $50 and $500. The lower-priced drones may not have video capabilities or GPS, which takes away from their effectiveness. Some drones also come equipped with controllers while others utilize mobile devices and apps. Most schools can start with a $100 drone for indoor use and a $300 drone for outdoor use to get their program off of the ground.

Controls

The controls for drones primarily come in two forms: app based or handheld. The handheld controllers for models still require the use of a mobile screen but offer the use of joysticks. App-based controllers are generally designed for the use of mobile devices or tablets.

There are obvious drawbacks for using a tablet such as an iPad, especially with younger students. The large size makes it hard to hold out in front of them while trying to execute the controls. Smaller units like cell phones will work better for smaller hands. Even for instructing older students or adults, a phone-sized screen is going to be the most comfortable and controllable. Devices smaller than eight inches will be most appropriate. Past models of smartphones (which are often wasting away in drawers) make a great option, as they can still download the apps via Wi-Fi, and there is not as much concern about using or breaking a teacher's or student's phone.

On the other side of device size is the ability to show multiple people the view from the drone. On a small screen, it's a bit more work to share the screen view with others. This means that the handheld controller of choice should be tested on the students. Fortunately, it is an easy thing to switch, so it may even evolve, depending on the instructional activity.

The added benefit of having a controller that has joysticks and buttons is that it allows for operators to utilize their tactile senses. The screen-based apps can sometimes be hard for users to feel, while joysticks and buttons allow the user to sense how much touch or force to use when trying to move the drone midair. Based on experience, more teachers and students prefer to have a controller in their hands. This is likely because most individuals equate the controls to that of a video-game console. Even though it may be slight, the resistance on the controller allows the user to feel how much they are moving the drone, as opposed to guessing with an app on the screen.

Controller-based models still require that a phone or mobile device be connected to see the camera if live video streaming is an option, as well as for some other operations. Controllers generally have antennas that will extend the range between the operator and the drone, and a reliable connection is important when you have a drone hovering in the air. Plus, a loss of connection or control is unsettling for the user and can also result in damage to the drone. Controllers are usually associated with upper-end models, starting at about the $500 price point.

Some of the app-controlled drones have different controller settings. Usually these come in the form of a joypad or tilt control. In the joypad mode, it simulates an external joystick: dragging the virtual circle in the desired direction will result in the drone doing the correlated action. Conversely, the tilt mode allows the user to use their mobile device or tablet as one big joystick. The user holds a virtual button on the screen and then tilts the whole device as a gyro. Based on the authors' experience with hundreds of teachers and students, there is no clear winner. The choice of joypad or tilt modes comes down to user preference. Since it only takes seconds to switch, let users try both modes and experience what is best for them. The key to successful deployment is teachers and users being comfortable with the technology and keeping it controlled through the activity.

No matter the control type, users should try to keep the drone's front facing away from them, in the same direction they are facing. This will allow for more of an intuitive control of the device. If the drone's front is facing to the left of the user and the operator pushes forward, the drone will move left. This is one of the most difficult things for new users to understand and results in the majority of early crashes. Keeping an eye on user and drone alignment will aid in the safety for the drone, people, and obstacles.

Stability

All drones are designed to take off, hover, and fly, but it is how they respond to user control and maintain stability in the air that is another large consideration. Low-price-point drones, generally of the toy category, may not hover when the user lets go of the control. Most models that cost more than the $100 price point will return to a hover when the user lets go of the control. This is important for novice learners who are unfamiliar with the controls or are trying to learn how to fly. When the controls are released and a drone hovers in place, it teaches students to just release the controls when there is an issue or when the device starts to move in an unexpected manner.

The use of drones indoors can present a challenge regardless of the model. Ventilation systems and even air changes through open doors or windows can cause the drone to drift. Some of the upper-end models have a vision system that looks at the ground when GPS is not available. Depending on the model, the use of ground images or sensors to detect potential obstructions may be a feature of the device. The downside of this is that some of the imaging systems may not work when the ground does not have distinct features; so something like a cafeteria or gym floor that does not have markings may not let it function correction. These types of sensors are subject to the right conditions and do not always work as intended; they should not be relied on as the only crash-prevention method.

Figure 4.1 Students flying a drone during a lesson in their school gymnasium

Generally, during indoor use, there is little that can be done to compensate for drift. This is compared to using the drone outside, where there is likely to be a wind condition to some extent. Even on calm days, once a drone gets up off the ground, it will likely encounter some level of wind. Advanced models with GPS assistance can hold the camera stable even in high winds. The compensation uses the motors to hold the unit stationary. Visually, the drone may be tilted into the wind, but it remains in the same position. If there is a gimbal (a mount that allows the camera to pivot on several axis so that that the picture is steady and level) on the camera, media can remain relatively high quality.

A GPS-enabled model is strongly recommended for flying outdoors. This feature adds an additional layer of safety and control, as well as stabilizing the unit in winds. Units without GPS can drift and end up in unintended places, potentially harming the unit, property, or even people. Drones with GPS usually have a return-home feature that will bring the unit back to where it took off. This feature is also critical if there is a loss of connection between the drone and the controller. In this event, the drone will return to the place it took off as long as it still has a GPS signal. Drones without GPS are great for indoor activities, but taking them outside risks a loss of control and/or a loss of the device. It is a good idea to only have experienced users take non-GPS models outdoors. Remember that there is still a risk of a flyaway (meaning the loss of the drone) if the control connection is lost.

Regardless of the model, there should be some type of foam bumper or propeller protectors when flying the drone inside. This will prevent contact from the blades with walls or people. It also prevents a significant amount of damage to the drone's gears and blades. Some models include foam hulls or bumpers with the initial purchase, while others require a separate purchase.

Media Quality

Aside from the GPS and the controller, the quality of the camera and media produced adds to the major price difference in drones. Some models have the ability to take 4K (resolution) video; and there are some models that have three different camera options (a price difference of nearly a thousand dollars). If you are not planning on producing high-quality video or media projects, then a lesser camera may be a cost-saving measure worth exploring.

Look at how the camera is mounted in the unit too. Some lower-cost models have fixed cameras that face forward and/or down. This gives the user a single perspective on the object that they want to take a picture of while in the air.

The inability to angle the camera presents a challenge when trying to get the best view or picture. This then requires more maneuvering or distance from the object. Some models offer the ability to have a mounted camera rotate up and down within a fixed directional housing, improving the ability to take pictures but not necessarily offering the best option as the camera is still limited on angle and direction.

The best cameras are mounted on what is called a gimbal system. This allows the camera to rotate and move as needed to capture the images. Gimbals stabilize the camera, even in harsh conditions. If a drone has a gimbal and GPS, it can stay stabilized in a strong wind and still capture quality video or images. Gimbal-based units give the operator control over the angle of capture from straight horizontal down to directly vertical. These types of mounts automatically stabilize the camera in any direction and even compensate for the vibrations of the drone. This movement, coupled with the ability to change altitude and distance from an object, is the best option for capturing a high-quality, professional-grade picture. Some higher-end models lift the drone's feet above the camera after takeoff, offering a 360-degree pan. However, in general, gimbal systems just pan from straight down to straight out.

Some drones provide external camera mounts for additional equipment, like a GoPro. Though this may save on the cost of camera equipment at first, it adds another layer of technical knowledge required. Additionally, not all separately mounted cameras enable a live stream of images; so the operator has to guess at what they are actually seeing, then land and check as necessary. In this scenario, extra battery life and time are required just to check on the images that were captured.

Some drones offer a media playback option, which lets the user replay the video or see the picture that was just taken. If the objective of the drone is to capture images, this offers the ability to make an instant decision on whether more media capturing needs to take place or if what has been obtained is sufficient for use.

The use of the camera is something that will likely be a selling point for many educators and administrators, so it is important to understand the differences in application prior to selecting a particular model. In the search for a drone, there will be countless online forums and editorials about the top selections. Look at what is really needed for the intended application and narrow your options. It is usually better to invest a bit more for quality than to experience buyer's remorse because a lower-quality unit proves to be insufficient or unreliable.

Storing images and videos occurs differently on various models. Some models require the user to have an external memory card or USB storage drive. Others enable the transfer from internal memory to the control device through the Wi-Fi connection. The use of a wireless transfer may seem like a good idea, but when there are larger files, especially video, this may take some time to transfer to the mobile device. In addition, storage on the mobile device may not handle the multiple large files that are created while flying. An external memory card allows for maximum storage and can be easily swapped out.

Data

As models start to distinguish themselves, another consideration is the type of information or data logging the drone is capable of providing. This is especially important to the application of concepts and the collection of data required to perform mathematical calculations. Non-GPS models will generally have, at minimum, the height that they are off the ground, but on some less expensive models, this does not exist either. More complex models will require you to create an account to activate the data logging, but this will record speed, altitude, and crashes automatically. GPS-equipped models can also track the location of the device and display coordinates or draw lines on a map. Another feature that GPS offers is the ability to gain accurate measurements of how high the drone is, how far from the operator (in regard to a straight line on the ground), and the line-of-sight distance from the operator to the drone. This serves as a pretty good demonstration and proof of concept for teaching the Pythagorean theorem, for example.

Unit of measurement can be an issue depending on the purpose and grade level of intended use. The primary unit of measurement is in metric units for most drones, and some allow for a quick app-based switch to U.S. standard units. Having metric measurements might be advantageous for some applications, but if the classroom is traditionally using standard units, purchasing a unit that operates in standard units should be a priority. There are some third-party piloting apps available that allow users to switch between metric and standard, but it should be noted that third-party apps have the potential to have unknown or unvetted flaws in them. It is not recommended that operators hack or use applications like this unless they are experienced users and understand the potential risks.

Batteries and Replacement Parts

Battery life is an important factor when selecting a drone. The amount of time that a device can remain in the air will impact how much students will be able to use it during instructional activities. Most drones have a flight time of around 20 minutes per charge and then require 40 to 90 minutes to recharge. This is something to think about in regard to the type of activities and amount of extra batteries to have on hand. It is a good rule to have one spare battery per drone if not several, depending on the cost.

And what happens to the drone when the battery runs out of juice? Some advanced units feature a built-in warning, an automatic return to takeoff point, or an automatic landing when battery life gets low. It is important to consider what will happen if you are going to fly over a pond during a science project, for example; you do not want the drone to end up in the water if the battery gets low. This isn't really an issue if the intended use is indoors.

During the purchase process, the availability of parts and support should also be examined. Due to institutional purchasing procedures, there are requirements that only approved vendors are used. Some vendors will sell the drone but not the extra propellers or batteries. If the drone is used indoors, there is a good chance that purchasing an extra propeller will be required. It is a good practice to purchase a spare set along with the new drone, to minimize down time. (There is bound to be that inadvertent bump that will damage a propeller.) Fortunately, propellers are inexpensive and easily replaced within minutes.

Foam bumpers are another consumable part of the drone. If the bumper or indoor hull is affordable, then it is easy to have on hand for replacement. If not, superglue is a very handy solution. Most of the indoor hulls can be easily repaired this way.

Like most technology, drones continue to change and evolve, becoming more user friendly as technological advancements are made. The selection of the device should consider the intended application. The worst-case scenario is the purchase of technology that does not adequately meet the needs of the instructor or the students and goes unused in a cabinet.

As with any educational program, there is a balancing act of quality and affordability based on the features required. The criteria outlined in this chapter should serve as a good guide to ensure that the selected drone will meet the expectations of the users. The main goal is to get technology that will engage, inspire, and motivate students to explore and learn in a new way.

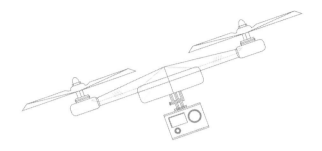

CHAPTER 5

Active Learning: Classroom Implementation

There are many considerations for the teacher looking to use drones with their students. Safety is paramount in any drone lesson or activity. Along with overall safety of the students and the space where the drones will be flying, there are requirements and safety aspects to each type of drone. This chapter looks at beginner, intermediate, and advanced drones and what to look for with each of them.

Safety

The most important consideration when using drones in the classroom is safety and the related issues that surround the operation of these technologies. With a device that has this magnetic effect for students, it is critical that instructors lay out a safety-and-operation plan prior to implementing it. During one demonstration of drones for an elementary school, a principal took a drone and hovered it over students who were seated. Of course, the students wanted to reach up and touch it. Had they done so, however, they would have injured their fingers if they encountered the blades. Lack of responsibility may not always be with students; adults need to have an understanding of the situation. If a drone's propeller makes contact with someone's hands or fingers, the results are not going to be good.

In the unfortunate event that blades do strike fingers or body, in most cases they just sting ; then the drone realizes it has struck something and shuts down its motors (There are settings that will not allow for this to happen, so be aware of your drone's safety features prior to use.) This is not to say that the drone could not cause more damage to younger students or to an eye. On the contrary, there is a reported case of a young girl being injured by a homemade drone. These ideas are not meant to scare users but to present the reality of drone operation, so you take the necessary steps to avoid negative consequences.

The number-one rule for safe drone operation is to avoid people, keeping a safe distance between the flying drone and other humans at all times. Whether the drone is overhead or simply nearby, operators should not fly close to people, as drones can shift or drift based on conditions. In a classroom setting, it is best to move all students a safe distance behind the operator and have as much distance between the operator and the drone as possible. If using the drone in the classroom, this may be more difficult, but the more room to make mistakes the better. Most drones come with indoor hulls made of foam or hard plastic, or you can buy these as accessory items. These bumpers are a must-have when using the drone indoors, as there is no contact with the propeller should the drone bump into a human. Additionally, the bumpers minimize the damage to drone motors and propellers, saving both time and money.

Having room for the drone to move is a key consideration even when the unit is just hovering. In a school building, opening doors, windows, and ventilation vents can change air pressures or cause air to move unexpectedly. Usually the movement is minimal and the drone recovers, but if the drone is close to an object, it may be damaged if it hits a wall or something else that is hard. When operating indoors, the drone will not have GPS mode to compensate for these types of changes.

Outdoor users will quickly see how much wind affects the flight of the drone. If the drone came with indoor hulls or bumpers, they should be removed when taking it outside. The excess foam will cause more drag and make the drone get rocked around by the air more.

The same idea of avoiding potential hazards indoors should be followed outside as well. And using the drone outside presents more hazards than in a classroom or gymnasium, where the drone is boxed in. There are a lot more risks of where the drone could go (buildings, cars, wires, trees) and numerous uncontrollable environmental factors. A quick internet search will show videos of drones gone rogue, flying away when they lose a connection to the operator. This problem was primarily an issue that occurred in early and less-expensive models. Again, the big factor is movement of air. Fortunately, some models have GPS features that will allow them to remain stable in the strongest winds; however, if the drone does not have this feature, it can get blown around and be nearly impossible for the user to control. New or inexperienced users tend to get scared at this point, but it is an opportunity to teach users how to remain calm and think through the problems. A good rule of thumb is to simply avoid outside flight if there is a high wind.

Appendix B provides a sample safety checklist for users to follow prior to flight. Having a checklist makes users cognitively process potential threats or risks ahead of time and conduct an assessment of how to avoid these potential issues. Striking a tree at 100 feet is going to result in more damage to equipment than a five-foot strike using a bumper in a gym. This, again, returns to the notion that knowledge of equipment and control of the aircraft require practice.

A comparison of models enables users to make an informed decision about safety and other variables prior to purchasing a drone. To assist with this process, the following three sections group models based on ease of use, price, and features. This is not meant to be an all-inclusive list of drones available in the retail market, but it does evaluate the models based on the experience of their use in the K–12 setting. Many new models are being developed and older models are being updated, so these sections focus on some of the more popular models in schools today. When it comes to name brands in drones, DJI and Parrot are two of the leaders. Although there are other manufacturers, the prominence of these two makers generally overshadows the others.

Beginner Models

Because there are numerous small drones and minidrones, buyers should use caution to avoid purchasing minis that are essentially just toys. The Rolling Spider and Airborne Cargo models from Parrot are small drones that have great control, maneuverability, and relatively safe operation. Both models are based off of the same platform, but their exterior structures are slightly different. The Spider is advantageous because it has two large wheels to protect itself in crashes; when it hits a wall or falls to the ground, it just bounces and is ready to go. These wheel bumpers are a great asset for younger students. The Air Cargo is designed for connecting blocks to the device, so it is excellent for demonstrating the impact of weight on lift or speed.

Both models have a camera that faces directly down, and both are controlled through an app that must be installed on a cell phone or tablet and connects through Bluetooth. They are highly recommended due to their stability and resiliency. Right out of the box, these models offer reliable, user-friendly options for younger students. Additionally, the ability to modify the operating systems of these two drones gives advanced-programming students a unique platform to see how code affects an actual object. Since the abstract nature of code can be boring, having a physical, interactive representation of students' work is inspiring.

These models have potential at both ends of the educational spectrum; your choice is just dependent on the need of the user. The price is below the $100 mark, so it is relatively affordable; and the app download is free and available on multiple devices. This is the same app that is used with some other Parrot products, like the Bebop as well. Flight time is only about eight minutes per battery, but batteries are inexpensive and easily changed. These models should be purchased with an external charger and a several spare batteries.

Intermediate Models

Intermediate models are classified as having more advanced features than the beginner models but are not necessarily professional grade. The two devices that have been used extensively in the K–12 setting are the Parrot AR.Drone 2.0 and Bebop. These two drones are a step up from the minidrones and come with more options.

The AR drone is the largest model that will be discussed here. It features forward- and downward-facing cameras, and uses app-based controls that need to be downloaded onto a mobile device that connects to a Wi-Fi signal. The quality of the front camera is fair and the downward-facing camera is grainy; but as a step up from the minidrones, this is where operators start receiving live video from the drone to the controlling device, offering live perspective and in-the-moment photographic capabilities—an impressive feature to be able to show students.

Video and images from the drone can either be stored on an internal USB drive or sent to the mobile device. The only issues relate to sending the images to a mobile device; you have to keep in mind that there needs to be enough space on the receiving device to receive large files, and large files can take an extended period to transfer over Wi-Fi. Also, after extensive use, there have been some connectivity issues while using this drone, especially when multiple drones are being used simultaneously.

The propellers on the AR are the hardest to change on any model reviewed here, requiring a special tool. However, they do come with a comprehensive indoor foam hull that acts like a 360-degree bumper. This model has proven to be fairly resilient, surviving many bumps and bruises. And the foam bumper can be glued and taped, and ready to fly again without much delay.

The Bebop is a favorite of teachers and students when using a drone indoors. This drone is smaller than the AR and handles much better, with a noticeable increase in response and speed in comparison. The Bebop also comes with GPS. This is not a major issue if using the drone indoors, but it does expand the user's ability to record data, conduct measurements, and create preset flights outdoors. The camera is a fish eye, which gives a 180-degree field of view. The downside is that indoor bumpers do not provide 360-degree protection; they leave the front relatively exposed and have to be purchased separately. However, the smaller blades on this model are easy to change and seem to be more durable than the ones on the AR.

The Bebop has the option to be flown by a handheld controller or by an app. But even with a controller, a mobile device is still needed to see live images. As discussed previously, handheld controls provide the added benefit of increased use of tactile senses and a better feeling of user control. But adding the controller is about $200 more.

Both the AR and Bebop have about a 20-minute flight time, depending on use, with batteries that are charged externally. This makes it easy to keep a spare charged and ready to go. On both models, it is recommended to purchase spare propellers as well. In the case of the AR, purchase a spare propeller kit, which has the lock washers, gear, and propellers—the parts most-often damaged—all in one place. The price of the AR.Drone 2.0 is approximately $250 while the Bebop is near $500.

Advanced Models

The DJI Phantom is the top-of-the-line model in this section. The Phantom line comes in four options: Phantom 3 Standard, Phantom 3 Advanced, and Phantom 3 Professional, followed by the Phantom 4. The Phantom 3 differences are primarily based on the camera system. All three models have a gimbal-mounted camera, but the Professional and Advanced models offer higher-quality media capturing. The Standard and Advanced comes with 2.7K video capability and a 12 MB camera, while Professional and Phantom 4 both have 4K video capabilities. The Standard camera is the only one manufactured by Panasonic; the others are made by Sony. The data is stored on a mini–memory card, and the user is still able to view the media on the device connected to the remote. This allows the operator to review media that is captured while the drone is still in position, giving the option to capture additional shots prior to landing.

The Phantom 3 is the ideal choice for flying outdoors, as it has GPS and the gimbal-mounted camera. The drone can hover in place even in a high wind and still capture high-quality media. Meanwhile, the GPS returns the drone home (the takeoff point) if it loses its signal or if the operator hits the related button on the controller (Advanced and Professional models). The GPS also enables the user to create a very detailed flight log that has information on distance, altitude, speed, and associated media files. The Phantom has the ability to create a map based on the data logging as well.

Though the controller is included in the price of each device, the controller still requires the operator to use a mobile device with an app to watch live video and execute some of the controls and options. And the mobile device needs to be physically connected to the controller through a wire. The Standard model has a slightly different remote than the others, which does not have as many options as the advanced models. The missing options are primarily camera controls and a return-to-home button.

The Phantom 4 has the same features of the Phantom 3 Professional but offers the added benefit of increased autonomous systems to avoid objects. This improves safety and reduces the likeliness of damage to the drone. On the other hand, the Phantom 3 Advanced and Professional models have a vision system feature that enables the drone to stay in place even without GPS. (GPS isn't always effective, as the ground image requires surfaces that have distinct features. Gym floors and water may be too smooth, for example.) However, the Phantom line is usually recommended for outdoor use, as they are more powerful and louder than other models. A Phantom's speed and power make flying one like driving a race car in a parking lot: there just is not enough room to let them do what they do! There are protectors for propellers available if the intention is to fly indoors, but this is something that should not be considered optional.

The batteries for the Phantom 3 will last approximately 25 minutes while the Phantom 4 will afford a few more minutes of additional flight time. The batteries are removable, but since they are considered intelligent batteries, they come at a cost of more than $100 each. The purchase price at the time of this book's printing ranges from $500 for the Phantom 3 Standard to $1300 for the Phantom 4. The price difference is based on the camera system. If high-quality images are the priority, then a model with a 4K camera is ideal; but if the goal is to have all the features and capture good images, then the Standard model will be sufficient.

As with any technology, the drone market is continually evolving. The prices have been decreasing as the technology is becoming more widely used, and there are more players offering various models. The competitive pricing and technological advances are advantageous for those who are looking to buy; and even well-equipped models offer severe price cuts when they are no longer the newest editions.

The choice of a drone depends on what is going to be effective in the classroom and still offer the best return on investment for the purchase price. If a small minidrone will accomplish the objective, then an Airborne Cargo or Rolling Spider will be a good choice. The Parrot AR drones are resilient, but they tend to be a bit bulky. The Bebop is a good choice too, but for the price difference, it is hard to pass up the Phantom. Ideally, having several options would be great, but if the drone is going to be used indoors, the Bebop has the slight edge; outdoors, the Phantom line is hard to beat. As new models and companies emerge, it is best to read reviews and forums prior to purchase, as it is not always beneficial to be the first one to buy something that has not had all the bugs worked out of it yet.

User Training

The successful implementation of drones into an educational setting is based on the training that end users receive. To take a technology such as this and just hand it to someone straight out of the box, without proper guidance, is not likely to produce advantageous results. If there is going to be an investment in new technology, administrators need to support the rollout of new technologies with sustainable professional development.

Unlike most technologies, the use of drones in the classroom presents a potential risk and liability. The key to safe operation is to have a skilled end user who is knowledgeable about the device that they are utilizing. Just as someone who is instructing a driver's education class must know how to safely use the car, classroom teachers using drones must have the same skill and expertise in operating their tools. There is no replacing flight time; so, prior to using a drone with others, it is critical that educators spend an extensive amount of time behind the controls.

The key to learning is finding a large open space without obstructions in which you can practice with the drone. Starting to fly in small spaces such as a classroom can be frustrating, and can lead to crashes and potential drone damage. The best place to start is in the school gymnasium. Unlike practicing outdoors, the drone is kept in a controlled environment this way and cannot get out of the enclosed space.

Inevitably, there will be a crash; but many models have external skeletons or bumpers to prevent damage, especially to blades. It is a good guideline for users to start flying at a low altitude. If there is a crash at three feet as opposed to 15, the drone will likely remain unharmed. Most crashes are generally associated with a lack of control. Speed and response settings should be turned down for new users—almost every drone has a setting for how fast it will accelerate or climb. Turning down these settings will give new users the ability to control and respond to potential issues at an accessible speed.

For the most part, drones will yaw up, and return to a hover when the operator lets go of the controls. A lot of times, individuals will freeze and stay on the sticks, which either causes a crash and/or increases the impact of a crash. Curiosity and the need to test the limits of the equipment appear even with teachers, so sometimes people purposely get close to obstacles or try to go fast. With the exception of drone racing (more about that in Chapter 8), the objective of the drone is to move to and obtain media or data that could not otherwise be collected.

As part of the drone implementation process, administrators should enact a set of procedures to distribute the drones and to report damage. Most parts are replaceable, and some vendors will replace or exchange a drone that has been damaged. The situation that needs to be avoided is a drone that is returned damaged by one teacher and cannot be used by the next teacher for their lesson. Having a simple sign-out sheet and process to report issues will alleviate unreported damage like this. Especially in the learning stages, there should be a reasonable expectation that some damage may occur. Conversely, administrators should not punish teachers for exploring new technologies as long as they do no use them in a reckless manner. If someone has not crashed a drone, they have not flown it long enough. Ideally, an instructional coach or administrator takes the lead on having oversight of the devices and keeps track to ensure that they remain operational.

The number-one cause of crashes is orientation of the drone. The easiest way to operate a drone is to make sure that the front (usually noted by the camera orientation) is facing away from the user—that the drone is facing in the same direction as the user. In this setup, regardless of whether the control is a hand controller or a phone app, the drone will go forward when the forward command is given. Oftentimes, once this orientation is changed and the front of the drone is angled in another direction, the operator can become confused and the chances of a crash increase. For example, when the front of the drone is facing to the left of the operator, forward command now sends the drone to the left of the operator. One of the easiest solutions is to reorient the drone so that it is once again facing in the same direction as the user—to maintain intuitive control of the device—and then move to the objective. Once at the objective, move the drone to capture the media and, prior to returning or moving it to another location, reorient the drone so that the front is once again away from the operator.

If given the option, select a drone with a controller that is separate from the app on a tablet or cell phone. The ability to hold joysticks is more comfortable to users than holding on a phone or tablet. The physical action allows operators to use their tactile senses and truly feel the movement of the controls.

As with any classroom implementation of technology, the teacher needs to be trained and knowledgeable about the technology to effectively utilize it in the classroom. In the case of drones, this is even more critical to ensuring safety of operation while using them with students. To that extent, operators should be able to do the following 10 steps prior to using a drone in the classroom:

1. Attach and remove the propellers

2. Connect the battery and power

3. Navigate the app and/or utilize the controller

4. Identify potential risks or hazards

5. Create a safe area for the drone to operate

6. Establish a connection between the controller and the drone

7. Take off and land successfully at least 10 times

8. Navigate the inside perimeter of a classroom three times within three feet of the wall

9. Navigate in and out of a classroom door 10 times

10. Move to five locations and hover

These skills are a good baseline for using a drone in the classroom. After conducting numerous professional-development trainings and observing teachers' use of these devices in the classroom, the 10 items listed have proven to be the essentials for creating a safe classroom where the technology is effectively used to assist with student learning. Without these prerequisite skills, teachers either cause a disruption to the classroom or risk student well-being. As this field is still emerging, there is no standardized set of proficiencies required to be certified in operation at the amateur level; again, these 10 skills serve as a baseline rather than a mastery level. Using a drone in an outdoor environment should include instruction on FAA regulations as well as outdoor safety. Expert flying of drones requires certification. Flying commercial drones requires operators to have, at minimum, a sport or recreational pilot's license.

Another critical element when training new users is to have an objective or a task. When adult learners have the ability to operate the drone, they will often push the limits, resulting in crashes and damages to the drone. When individuals are left without guidance, they try things like landing on a basketball hoop, seeing how close to the ceiling they can get, or trying to fly over other people. Any training or activity should be goal focused so that participants are trying to accomplish a task rather than openly exploring the limits of the drone.

Storyboards

A storyboard is a sequential combination of written and graphical representation of the media that is going to be captured or created in a video, animation, or other motion graphics. This allows the user to visually organize media elements that they will need to complete the production. It is typically used in creating media for video or media productions but has an essential role in drone operations: it allows users to visually map out how they will use the drone.

Creating a storyboard serves the purpose of ensuring the drone is used for an exact purpose and captures the correct data that the user wants to collect. The visualization guides the operator so that they know exactly what they have to accomplish while the drone is in the air. This is important if there are students operating the drone, as they have a focused plan instead of just playing or experimenting with the drone, which could lead to issues. Additionally, due to the limited resources of time and technology, using a storyboard speeds up the process of collecting data. There is a finite amount of class time, and having a plan to gather the appropriate data ensures that this is done in an expeditious manner. A focused plan also allows for effective deployment of a drone (it is doubtful that there will be a one to one ratio in the classroom). The other factor is battery life, which is usually around 20 to 30 minutes, depending on type of drone and usage.

Figure 5.1 Students preparing for a drone activity in their school gymnasium.

Storyboards can be completed in several ways, including print and digital. Appendix C has a sample storyboard that can be used or modified to match the type of usage. Considerations should include the height of the drone, the angle of the camera (if applicable), the speed of the drone, and the requirements for video or still imagery. The easiest thing to do is just print out copies of the storyboard and have students pencil in their plans. This allows the students to quickly create the storyboard so that they have a physical reference point when it comes time to actually fly the drone.

Common Issues and Resolutions

In this section, there will be discussion of some of the most common issues experienced when trying to fly a drone. The majority of these issues are only introduced after the drone has had a crash or hard landing, or has struck something. With that in mind, when ordering the drone, seriously consider buying some replacement parts, such as blades, spare batteries, and tools. There are spare parts listed in the manual for a reason, as it is common to see these items damaged or needing replacement. There is a nominal cost in having spare parts on hand, but based on experience, it is frustrating to need these and not have them available. Also, when ordering the actual drone, find out if the vendor can get these types of parts. Some vendors will sell the drones but not the supporting materials. Depending on the seller and the procurement process, getting spare parts may not be as simple as going to an online store and just clicking "add to cart."

There are many videos available about every drone that is commercially available. Referring to YouTube is a common approach for learning more about issues and resolutions that others have had. No matter what, you are not the first person to have an issue. There is generally someone (or multiple people) who have had similar challenges and have found resolutions. Most of the major manufacturers have forums where users of their products can come together and form a collective online knowledge base.

Lack of Connectivity

The most common issue that occurs is a drone that will not connect to the control device. This occurs more often when there is an app-based control on a phone or tablet. There are several possibilities for issues on both the drone and the phone or tablet. These types of devices use Wi-Fi sent from the drone to the mobile device. First, users should check that they are connected to the correct drone, especially if there are multiple units in the vicinity. If a connection still cannot be established, go back to basics and restart everything. This means unplugging the battery from the drone and closing the app on the phone, and perhaps even restarting the phone as well. After doing a whole system and controller reboot, connectivity is usually restored.

Lack of connectivity occurs more often when trying to switch between multiple users on the same drone. Additionally, some devices will automatically connect to the drone, as it remembers the Wi-Fi. The best practice is to use a single device, when possible, to control the drone, minimizing the risk of this issue.

Drone Not Lifting or Stabilizing

After a hard landing or crash, there is a chance that damage has occurred to the equipment. Although drones are generally durable and can survive numerous crashes, each event is unique. If the drone is not stabilizing or has a hard lean to one side, it is time to do some investigating. Do not operate the drone without first finding a solution, as more damage may occur.

A visual inspection of the bumpers and blades is usually the first place to look. In a quadcopter, the side and angle that the drone unexpectedly moves in is likely the culprit. Even small dings in the blade that look minor may be the cause. This is where it is essential to have a few spare blades on hand so you can quickly switch them out.

The bumpers can usually operate with some damage and even broken pieces; however, the hull may be the problem. You can check the hull by either removing it or changing it if there is another unit available with the same model. New foam hulls can be expensive, but most damaged hulls are easily fixed with some superglue. Though the hulls tend to take a great deal of abuse and damage, with some glue, they can still remain operational.

On some models, there is a feature to check for issues and to recalibrate the motors. If your model is equipped with this feature, a notification will appear on the app after a crash. This can serve two purposes, either recalibrating the motors to stabilize flight or indicating which prop is having the issue. If there is a problem identified with one of the blades, switch it out if there is a spare available. If no spare is present, switch the blade with the one that is diagonal. There are two types of blades on each drone, so make sure that it is the correct orientation. Swapping the blades will at least enable the identification or isolation of the problem to confirm it is a blade issue.

When issues occur, it is important to keep a cool head and just work through the problem. If it happens during class time, embrace the opportunity to turn students into problem solvers and researchers. Working with technology means that issues will undoubtedly arise, so there needs to be a solid understanding and mental preparation. If students are of the appropriate age, the problems that occur could create an important incidental learning situation.

Plan ahead for problems by having at least one spare battery, a set of props, and a tool kit if one is needed to remove the blades. This way, the resolution of issues doesn't impact instructional time for long.

GPS Calibration

GPS models have their own set of issues, including calibration—the turning of the drone on its axis. Just note that if the screen keeps requiring you to calibrate it, you may need to try a new area to operate the drone. Although some models are designed to be used indoors without GPS, it is impossible to fly without calibration and can be frustrating for users to figure out. If this happens, just try a different location, as it may be an electromagnetic interference from the building or structure.

- **CCSS.ELA-Literacy.W.3.2:** Write informative/explanatory texts to examine a topic and convey ideas and information clearly.

ABSTRACT

This lesson concentrates on the cardinal directions (north, south, east, and west). The teacher will give a lesson on the cardinal directions and then students will work in groups to complete an activity. During this activity, students will devise a route to get from a starting point to an end point utilizing all of the cardinal directions. They will write this route on an index card. While the students are working, the teacher will line sentence strips on the floor to replicate the map. Students will assess one another by switching cards with another group. As a hands-on activity, students will navigate a drone to demonstrate the route.

OBJECTIVE

Interpret simple maps and use cardinal directions (north, south, east, and west) to devise a route.

MATERIALS

- "Neighborhood" map with a "start" and "end" point circled
- Index cards
- Sentence strips with street names
- Drone

PROCEDURES

- The teacher gives a lesson on cardinal directions.
- Students are broken into groups.
- Teacher distributes a "neighborhood" map to each group with different "start" and "end" points circled.
- The teacher distributes index cards to each group.
- The teacher references the posted directions.

- The puppy got loose! Luckily, there was a police officer who saw the puppy dig under a fence. The police officer followed the puppy, finally retrieving him after many blocks and several turns. You are the police officer following the puppy. Using cardinal directions, write the route you took to retrieve the puppy.
  All cardinal directions must be used.

- Groups of students work collaboratively to devise the route that the police officer took to retrieve the puppy. *Example:* The puppy traveled half of a block east on Grace Street. Once the puppy reached the corner, the puppy traveled two blocks south. The puppy then rounded the corner and went west two blocks. At that corner, the puppy ran north one and a half blocks until the police officer caught up with it. What is the name of the street where the puppy was found?

- Students write the route on the index card.

- Students demonstrate understanding of learning by participating in a drone activity.

- An assessment concludes the lesson.

MODIFICATION

The puppy rounds three corners before being retrieved.

DRONE ACTIVITY

- The teacher lines the floor with sentence strips to represent the neighborhood map.

- Students switch index cards with another group.

- Using a drone, students model the route on the index card: The drone is placed on the starting point. A student reads the first direction aloud. Another student uses the drone to travel the given direction along the floor map, landing the drone at the correct location.

- The student hands the drone controller to one of their group members. A different student reads the next direction aloud while that group member flies the drone along the route.

- The process continues until all directions are completed.

- The group who wrote the directions verifies if the route was followed correctly.

ASSESSMENT

Students switch their index cards with another group. Each group uses the drone to model the written directions.

MODIFICATION

The puppy rounds three corners before being retrieved.

ENRICHMENT

The puppy rounds five or more corners before being retrieved.

LESSON PLAN

DRONE WARFARE

CONTENT
Social Studies

GRADE SPAN
Middle School

COMMON CORE STATE STANDARDS ADDRESSED

- **CCSS.ELA-Literacy.RH.6-8.1:** Cite specific textual evidence to support analysis of primary and secondary sources.

- **CCSS.ELA-Literacy.RI.6.1:** Cite textual evidence to support analysis of what the text says explicitly as well as inferences drawn from the text.

- **CCSS.ELA-Literacy.RI.8.1:** Cite the textual evidence that most strongly supports an analysis of what the text says explicitly as well as inferences drawn from the text.

- **CCSS.ELA-Literacy.W.6.1:** Write arguments to support claims with clear reasons and relevant evidence.

Additional Standards Addressed

- **CCSS.ELA-Literacy.RI.6.1**

- **CCSS.ELA-Literacy.RI.8.1**

ABSTRACT

This lesson concentrates on drone warfare. The teacher will give a lesson on the use of drones in war. Students will research drone warfare and decide on three articles they will use to cite contextual evidence. Students will participate in a class discussion, citing specific examples on how the United States uses drones as weapons of war. Students will engage in a hands-on drone activity, flying the drone into "enemy territory" and identifying enemy vulnerabilities. A discussion about the benefits of using drones for this purpose will follow. Teacher will randomly assign students a position to take in the argument centering on whether or not the use of drones is justifiable during combat. Students will write an argumentative essay in response to the prompt.

OBJECTIVE

- Cite textual evidence to support an argument.

- Develop an argumentative essay responding to the prompt.

MATERIALS

- Two classrooms (one labeled "United Stated of America" and the other "China")

- Paper (white and colored)

- Articles on drone warfare

- Representations of important landmarks (i.e., schools, hospitals, weapons factories, known enemy hideouts, and/or political landmarks). Students represent the landmarks by writing a description of the landmark on construction paper.

- Two drones

- CCSS Writing rubric

PROCEDURES

- Teacher gives a lesson on drone warfare.

- Students contribute what they have heard about drone warfare. The teacher records the responses.

- Students research drone warfare and decide on three articles they will use to cite contextual evidence to support their argument.

- Students participate in a drone activity.

- Students engage in class discussion on how the United States uses drones in warfare, referencing specific examples from their chosen articles.

- The teacher displays the prompt: The United States is in the midst of an aggressive battle against terrorism. While using drones in warfare has reduced the capabilities of terroristic organizations, they have also killed civilians. Contemplate whether it is more important to consider civilian lives or to focus on national security. Are drones a justifiable weapon of war?

- The teacher hands out the two types of paper to the students. The paper represents each student's stance pertaining to the question: white means that drones are a justifiable weapon of war and colored means that drones are not a justifiable weapon of war.

- Students construct a draft of an argumentative essay.

- Students switch drafts with someone of a different stance. Students' assess each other's drafts.

- Students make revisions on their drafts.

- An assessment concludes the lesson.

DRONE ACTIVITY

- Two separate classrooms participate. One is labeled the "United States of America" while the other is labeled "China."

- The important landmarks are spread out onto the respective floors of each classroom.

- Each class navigates their drone into the other room (enemy territory) to take surveillance video for analysis in their respective country.

- Students identify enemy vulnerabilities based on the drone surveillance footage.

ASSESSMENT

Students write an argumentative essay in response to the prompt. The teacher grades the essay with a rubric.

MODIFICATION

Students choose which stance to take on the prompt.

ENRICHMENT

Students debate the argument.

Science

LITTER CLASSIFICATION

CONTENT

Science

GRADE SPAN

Elementary School

COMMON CORE STATE STANDARDS ADDRESSED

- **CCSS.ELA-Literacy.RST.6-8.1:** Cite specific textual evidence to support analysis of science and technical texts.

- **CCSS.ELA-Literacy.RST.6-8.7:** Integrate quantitative or technical information expressed in words in a text with a version of that information expressed visually (e.g., in a flowchart, diagram, model, graph, or table).

- **CCSS.ELA-Literacy.W.3.1:** Write opinion pieces on topics or texts, supporting a point of view with reasons.

Additional Standards Addressed

- **CCSS.ELA-Literacy.W.3.1.a–d**

ABSTRACT

This lesson concentrates on identifying and analyzing the types of litter that pollute the environment. The teacher will explain how pollution has become a huge problem and has had negative effects on the environment. The teacher will also introduce the debates regarding climate change. Students will engage in a drone activity, using video footage taken by the drone to identify the litter they see. Then they will use six different categories to classify the litter (wood, paper, fabric, metal, glass, plastic). A group discussion will follow about the effects of litter on the environment. The lesson assessment will require students to write an opinion piece about what the earth will look like in 50 years and must include evidence from the students' research.

OBJECTIVE

- Classify different kinds of litter.

- Hypothesize and write an opinion piece about what the earth will look like in 50 years. The opinion piece must include evidence from the students' drone research.

MATERIALS

- Drone

- USB drive (one per group)
- Chart paper

PROCEDURES

- The teacher introduces the lesson, engaging the class in a discussion about litter and the effects litter has on the environment.
- Students participate in a drone activity, using its images to identify the types of litter they see in the environment (wood, paper, fabric, metal, glass, plastic).
- The teacher assigns each group a type of litter; then each group researches how long it takes for that piece of litter to break down. Students record research findings on their chart paper.
- The teacher displays the results of all groups' research on chart paper hung around the room. Students are invited to view each other's work.
- The teacher engages students in a class discussion about how long it takes each type of litter to break down and the long-term environmental effects.
- With their groups, students hypothesize what the earth will look like in 50 years.
- An assessment concludes the lesson.

DRONE ACTIVITY

- Students fly a drone around school property. They record video footage of litter on and around the premises.
- The teacher breaks students into groups.
- Each group transfers the drone footage to their USB drive.
- Each group watches the video several times. Students identify and record the litter they observed on the video.
- On chart paper, students classify the litter according to six categories: wood, paper, fabric, metal, glass, and plastic.

ASSESSMENT

Hypothesize and write an opinion piece about what the earth will look like in 50 years. The opinion piece must include evidence from students' research.

MODIFICATION

Students create an anti-litter poster.

ENRICHMENT

Students create an anti-litter poster in addition to writing an opinion piece about what the earth will look like in 50 years.

LESSON PLAN

SOLAR SYSTEM ANALYSIS

CONTENT

Science

GRADE SPAN

Middle School

COMMON CORE STATE STANDARDS ADDRESSED

- **CCSS.ELA-Literacy.RST.6-8.1:** Cite specific textual evidence to support analysis of science and technical texts.

- **CCSS.ELA-Literacy.RST.6-8.7:** Integrate quantitative or technical information expressed in words in a text with a version of that information expressed visually (e.g., in a flowchart, diagram, model, graph, or table).

- **CCSS.ELA-Literacy.RST.6-8.8:** Distinguish among facts, reasoned judgment based on research findings, and speculation in a text.

ABSTRACT

This lesson focuses on the solar system and continuing education to increase awareness of earth's environmental issues (pollution, climate change, etc.) and encourage preservation. The teacher will present a quick refresher of basic information about the planets in our solar system as well as about earth's moon. Students will build on their previous knowledge of the solar system, researching the planets (Mercury, Venus, Earth, Mars, Jupiter, Saturn, Uranus, Neptune) and their positions in space. Working in groups, students will develop their own questions on index cards for each planet. (Each planet will have a minimum of six higher-order-thinking questions.) Students will then exchange their cards with another group and participate in a related drone activity.

OBJECTIVE

- Identify and describe the characteristics of the solar system.
- Identify and describe the characteristics of each planet.
- Develop higher-order-thinking questions.

MATERIALS

- Index cards
- Solar system cutouts to place on the floor
- Drone

PROCEDURES

- The teacher gives a minilesson on the solar system.
- Students engage in a class discussion on what they know about the solar system.
- The teacher breaks students into groups.
- Students research the planets in the solar system.
- Working in their groups, students develop higher-order-thinking questions about the solar system, with a minimum of six questions

per planet. Students must cite textual evidence when devising the questions, and then transfer the questions to index cards. (The planet name is the answer to each question.)

- Each group exchanges their flash cards with another group.

- Students engage in a hands-on drone activity.

- Assessment is embedded in the drone activity.

DRONE ACTIVITY

- The teacher recreates the solar system on the floor with the planet cutouts.

- Groups exchange question cards with another group.

- The first group is called up. A student from the group reads the question on their first card and then discusses the answer with their group. Another student in the group flies the drone to the planet that answers the question. The students in their seats keep track of the questions; and if the question asked appears on the cards in front of them, it gets checked off so that it is not repeated.

- The group who wrote the description acknowledges if the answer is correct. If the answer is correct, the group with the drone is awarded a point in a running tally that the teacher keeps on the board.

- The student flying the drone passes the drone controller to another group member, and the student reading the description passes the remaining question cards to a different group member. This process repeats itself until all group members have been assessed.

- The procedure is the same for the remaining groups, and the teacher decides how many rounds the activity will last.

- In the event of a tie, the teacher devises a challenge question.

ASSESSMENT

Assessment is embedded in the drone activity.

MODIFICATION

Students develop three higher-order-thinking questions per planet.

ENRICHMENT

Students develop eight higher-order-thinking questions per planet.

Mathematics

SYSTEMS OF LINEAR EQUATIONS

CONTENT

Mathematics

GRADE SPAN

Middle School

COMMON CORE STATE STANDARDS ADDRESSED

- **CCSS.Math.Content.8.EE.C.7:** Solve linear equations in one variable.

- **CCSS.Math.Content.8.EE.C.8:** Analyze and solve pairs of simultaneous linear equations.

- **CCSS.Math.Content.HSA.REI.C.6:** Solve systems of linear equations exactly and approximately (e.g., with graphs), focusing on pairs of linear equations in two variables.

Additional Standards Addressed

- **CCSS.Math.Content.8.EE.C.7.a–b**

- **CCSS.Math.Content.8.EE.C.8.b–c**

ABSTRACT

This lesson concentrates on solving systems of linear equations. The teacher will give a lesson on linear equations and lead a class discussion in the different ways of solving systems of equations. Students will observe how two functions with the same variables are able to work together and then solve for the two unknown variables, using different methods to come up with solutions. Students will alternate flying a drone in a line for 30 feet and record the data. Using this data, students will write a linear equation and use multiple methods to solve it. Students will then work in groups to create system-of-equations word problems and answer keys for those problems, writing the word problems on index cards. Switching the index cards with a different group, students will assess each other by solving the problems and demonstrating the problems using the drone.

OBJECTIVE

Use a system of linear equations to demonstrate and solve real-life questions about flying drones.

MATERIALS

- Tape measure
- Timer
- Index cards
- Drone

PROCEDURES

- The teacher delivers a lesson on systems of linear equations.
- Students engage in a class discussion on the various methods of solving systems of equations.
- Students independently complete practice questions on solving systems of equations.
- The teacher divides students into groups.
- The student groups engage in a hands-on drone activity.
- After recording their data, students find the average rate for each situation.

- With their groups, students write a linear equation to represent the situation.

- Students create system-of-equations word problems with their groups. They set up situations to determine when one drone would catch another drone if using different starting points.

- Students write their group's word problems on index cards and create an answer key for them. The answer key shows different methods for solving systems of equations.

- A peer assessment of the word problems concludes the lesson.

DRONE ACTIVITY

- Students pick a starting point.

- Students use a tape measure to mark a spot 30 feet away from the starting point. This as the ending point.

- A student flies the drone for 30 feet while other members of the group time the flight and record the results.

- The process repeats until all members of the group have flown the drone.

ASSESSMENT

Each group switches their word-problem cards with another group. After successfully solving the problems, each group will demonstrate the problem using the drone.

MODIFICATION

Students demonstrate the word problems their own group created.

ENRICHMENT

Students write about the outcomes of the assessment.

ESTIMATING AND MEASURING UNITS OF LENGTH

CONTENT

Mathematics

GRADE SPAN

Elementary

COMMON CORE STATE STANDARDS ADDRESSED

- **CCSS.MATH.CONTENT.2.MD.A.1:** Measure the length of an object by selecting and using appropriate tools such as rulers, yardsticks, meter sticks, and measuring tapes.

- **CCSS.MATH.CONTENT.2.MD.A.3:** Estimate lengths using units of inches, feet, centimeters, and meters.

- **CCSS.MATH.CONTENT.4.MD.A.1:** Know relative sizes of measurement units within one system of units including km, m, cm; kg, g; lb, oz.; l, ml; hr, min, sec. Within a single system of measurement, express measurements in a larger unit in terms of a smaller unit. Record measurement equivalents in a two-column table.

- **CCSS.Math.Content.5.MD.A.1:** Convert among different-sized standard measurement units within a given measurement system (e.g., convert 5 cm to 0.05 m), and use these conversions in solving multistep, real-world problems.

ABSTRACT

This lesson concentrates on student knowledge and application of estimation using different methods. The teacher will lead a refresher lesson on estimation (an educated guess based on one's opinion) and follow with a discussion about when to use customary units of length (inches, feet, yards). (The students will be familiar with measuring and estimated guessing.) Students will participate in a hands-on drone activity that will investigate estimation and then convert actual distances into customary units of length. Assessment is embedded in the drone activity.

OBJECTIVE

- Estimate measurements in feet and inches.
- Convert actual measurements into customary units of length.

MATERIALS

- Tape measure
- Drone

PROCEDURES

- The teacher gives a minilesson on estimating measurements.
- The teacher engages students in a class discussion on when it is appropriate to use certain customary units of length.
- Students give examples on when they would use inches, feet, and yards to measure.
- The teacher breaks up students into groups of four.
- Students participate in a drone activity.
- Assessment is embedded in the drone activity.

DRONE ACTIVITY

- Each student in the group is assigned a number: 1–4.
- Student 1 chooses any measurement (using feet and inches) up to 25 feet.
- Student 2 flies the drone to their estimated distance.
- The class gives a thumbs-up or thumbs-down to show whether or not they agree that the estimation was accurate.

- Students 3 and 4 use the tape measure to determine the actual distance of the drone flight and share this information with the class.

- The class converts the actual distance into yards, feet, and inches.

- After each round, students rotate so that each student in the group has a chance to estimate while flying the drone.

ASSESSMENT

Assessment is embedded within the drone activity.

MODIFICATION

Markers are placed every 10 feet to assist with estimation.

ENRICHMENT

Students find the difference between the actual measurement and estimated measurement.

Language Arts

LESSON PLAN

DRONE HISTORY AND OPERATION

CONTENT

Language Arts

GRADE SPAN

Middle School

COMMON CORE STATE STANDARDS ADDRESSED

- **CCSS.ELA-Literacy.W.8.2:** Write informative/explanatory texts to examine a topic and convey ideas, concepts, and information through the selection, organization, and analysis of relevant content.

Additional Standards Addressed

- **CCSS.ELA-Literacy.W.8.2.a–f**

ABSTRACT

This lesson concentrates on writing an informative essay on a topic relevant to digital-age skills: drones. Students will conduct research on drones in order to acquire background knowledge. Students will be expected to investigate the history of drones, safety precautions, rules, regulations, and current uses of drones. The teacher will engage students in a class discussion on the current state of robotics and drone usage, recording student responses on chart paper. Students will then participate in a hands-on drone activity as further research for writing their informative essay. This exercise will build essay-writing skills and strategies, and will include the procedure of flying a drone. The final essay will be assessed using a CCSS writing rubric.

OBJECTIVE

- Develop a topic (concerning drones) by using textual evidence to support a main idea.

- Write an informative essay about drones using relevant details from texts.

- Describe the steps in flying a drone.

MATERIALS

- Chart paper

- Drone

- CCSS Writing rubric

PROCEDURES

- Students are assigned to research drones to acquire background knowledge on a topic. This research should include the history of drones, drone safety, rules, regulations, and current uses of drones. Students are required to research a minimum of five articles.

- The teacher presents a minilesson on the current state of robotics.

- Students engage in a class discussion on the various uses of drones and determine how drones are useful in society.

- The teacher records their responses on chart paper.

- Students participate in a hands-on drone activity.

- Students write an informative essay that includes the procedure for flying a drone.

- A rubric assessment concludes the lesson.

DRONE ACTIVITY

- The teacher models how to fly a drone.

- A student practices a drone takeoff.

- The student flies the drone in a straight line across the room and then in reverse, back to the starting point.

- The student lands the drone.

- The process is repeated until all the students have flown the drone.

ASSESSMENT

Students write an informative essay that includes the procedure for flying a drone, and the teacher grades the essay using a CCSS Writing rubric.

MODIFICATION

Students explain the flying steps to each other before writing the essay.

ENRICHMENT

Students turn the drone around to return it to the starting point instead of flying it in reverse.

DRONES AND TEST MONITORING

CONTENT

Language Arts

GRADE SPAN

Middle School

COMMON CORE STATE STANDARDS ADDRESSED

- **CCSS.ELA-Literacy.W.6.1:** Write arguments to support claims with clear reasons and relevant evidence.

Additional Standards Addressed

- **CCSS.ELA-Literacy.W.6.1.a–e**

ABSTRACT

This lesson concentrates on writing an argumentative essay about drones, encouraging the development of logical ideas and a cohesive summary. The teacher will begin the lesson by introducing students to the idea of using drones to monitor students while taking tests, citing China as an example (China uses drones to detect participants who are cheating during the college entrance exam). The students will participate in a test-taking simulation in which they are randomly assigned cards that instruct them on how to behave during the activity. (The teacher will clarify beforehand that the test work-sheet will not count toward the students' grades; it is only a simulation.) After completing the drone activity (the test), students will watch the video and engage in a class discussion on what was captured and how they felt completing the worksheet. Students will then write an argumentative essay to convince the local board of education that drones should or should not be used to ensure academic integrity in the classroom.

OBJECTIVE

Write an argumentative essay convincing the local board of education that drones should or should not be used to ensure academic integrity in the classroom.

MATERIALS

- Article on China using drones to monitor their college entrance exam
- Index cards
- Worksheets (any subject)
- Drone

PROCEDURES

- The teacher introduces the concept of using drones to monitor participants during tests and exams, providing students with an article about how China is using drones to monitor its college entrance exam.

- The teacher explains the purpose of the test-taking simulation.

- Students engage in the drone activity by taking the tests.

- Following the test, students review the drone's video footage and have a class discussion about the experience of the simulation.

- Students draft a response to this prompt: China has used drones to become aware of participants cheating during *gaokao*, China's National Higher-Education Entrance Examination. Should drones be allowed to monitor test taking in schools to ensure academic integrity is upheld, or is this method too invasive? Plan and develop your point of view on this issue. Write an argumentative essay convincing your local board of education that drones should or should not be used to ensure academic integrity in the classroom.

- Students assess each other's drafts, analyzing the work to see if it contains effective persuasive techniques and providing meaningful feedback.

- Students revise their persuasive essays based on the peer assessment.

DRONE ACTIVITY

- The teacher explains to students that they are simulating a five-minute test-taking experience in which a drone records them throughout the activity.

- The teacher distributes a worksheet facedown to students. (The worksheet can pertain to any subject; the subject matter is not relevant to the activity.)

- The teacher distributes index cards facedown to students and explains that the students are to follow the directions on the index cards. The index cards list one of the following four things, indicating what each student should do during the activity:

  - Complete the worksheet.

  - Cheat: turn around several times during the assignment to look at another student's answers.

  - Cheat: pretend to check your left hand for answers several times during the assignment.

  - Cheat: several times during the assignment, pretend the answers are written on the inside of your notebook.

- The teacher begins flying the drone and instructs students to begin the activity.

- The teacher flies the drone above the students while they complete the worksheet.

- At the end of the five-minute activity, the teacher lands the drone.

- The teacher informs the class that the index cards had various instructions on them and that some of the index cards instructed students to pretend to cheat.

- The teacher plays the drone recording for the class.

- The teacher engages the students in a class discussion on what the drone captured on video, asking the students how they felt knowing the drone was recording them and if it affected their performance.

ASSESSMENT

Students assess each other's drafts, analyzing the work to see if it contains effective persuasive techniques and providing meaningful feedback.

MODIFICATION

Students debate the issue.

ENRICHMENT

The teacher assigns students to take a certain stance on the issue.

DRONES AND TRAFFIC SAFETY

CONTENT

Language Arts

GRADE SPAN

Middle School

COMMON CORE STATE STANDARDS ADDRESSED

- **CCSS.ELA-Literacy.RST.6-8.1:** Cite specific textual evidence to support analysis of science and technical texts.

- **CCSS.ELA-Literacy.RI.6.1:** Cite textual evidence to support analysis of what the text says explicitly as well as inferences drawn from the text.

- **CCSS.ELA-Literacy.RI.6.2:** Determine a central idea of a text and how it is conveyed through particular details; provide a summary of the text distinct from personal opinions or judgments.

- **CCSS.ELA-Literacy.RI.6.3:** Analyze in detail how a key individual, event, or idea is introduced, illustrated, and elaborated in a text (e.g., through examples or anecdotes).

- **CCSS.ELA-Literacy.W.6.2:** Write informative/explanatory texts to examine a topic and convey ideas, concepts, and information through the selection, organization, and analysis of relevant content

Additional Standards Addressed

- **CCSS.ELA-Literacy.W.6.2.a–f**

- **CCSS.Math.Content.6.EE.B.6**

- **CCSS.Math.Content.7.EE.B.4**

ABSTRACT

This lesson concentrates on creating safer conditions during the student drop-off procedure at school. The teacher will lead a discussion on the ways in which the current drop-off procedure works and could be improved (traffic patterns, congestion, pedestrian crossings, etc.). Students will use a drone's camera to film the impacted areas for one week (five school days) and study the video to assess the current procedures. The students will then develop recommendations to improve upon current practices and work in groups to create a poster about these improvements. They will also write a narrative essay about the environmental impact of biking or walking to school instead.

OBJECTIVE

- Identify areas that need improvement in the student drop-off procedure.

- Analyze the traffic patterns and parking lots to determine if there is a better design.

- Create a poster of proposed changes to the student drop-off procedure.

- Write a narrative essay in response to this prompt: what are the environmental benefits of students walking and cycling to school?

MATERIALS

- Drone

- Poster board

- CCSS Writing rubric

PROCEDURES

- The teacher leads the class in a discussion regarding the student drop-off procedure. The teacher polls the class to determine how many students are dropped off at school and how many students walk or ride their bicycles to school.

- The teacher surveys the students on their feelings of safety with the current drop-off procedure.

- The teacher explains that over a five-day time span, the students will participate in a drone activity.

- After completing the drone activity, students work in groups to create a poster about how the current student drop-off procedure can be improved.

- Students research the effects of car emissions on the environment, citing at least five articles.

- Each student writes a narrative essay in response to this prompt: what are the environmental benefits of students walking and cycling to school?

DRONE ACTIVITY

- Students shoot drone footage of the student drop-off area and surrounding area for one week. This occurs during peak morning drop-off times.

- At the end of the five-day drone activity, students view the drone footage. Working in groups, students identify areas needing improvement in the student drop-off procedure.

- Students analyze the traffic patterns and parking lots to determine if there is a better design for the existing areas.

- Still working with their groups, students create a poster of proposed changes to the student drop-off procedure.

ASSESSMENT

Students use a CCSS Writing rubric to assess each other's narrative essays.

MODIFICATION

The drone records for one day instead of five.

ENRICHMENT

Students write a proposal to the principal requesting to change the drop-off procedure. The proposal should include the safety risks of the current drop-off procedure and a prospective procedure that will remedy the risks.

Interdisciplinary

THE UNDERGROUND RAILROAD

CONTENT

Social Studies, Science, ELA, and Mathematics

GRADE SPAN

Middle School

COMMON CORE STATE STANDARDS ADDRESSED

- **CCSS.ELA-Literacy.RH.6-8.1:** Cite textual evidence to support analysis of what the text says explicitly as well as inferences drawn from the text.

- **CCSS.ELA-Literacy.RH.6-8.2:** Determine the central ideas or information of a primary or secondary source; provide an accurate summary of the source distinct from prior knowledge or opinions.

- **CCSS.ELA-Literacy.W.6.3.e:** Provide a conclusion that follows from the narrated experiences or events.

- **CCSS.MATH.CONTENT.7.RP.A.2:** Recognize and represent proportional relationships between quantities.

ABSTRACT

This lesson concentrates on the Underground Railroad. The teacher will give a lesson on the history of the Underground Railroad. Students will engage in a class discussion, identifying the risks and consequences of an escape attempt. Students will make generalizations about the Underground Railroad. Working in collaborative groups, students will research fugitive slaves and map out their journey to freedom. This will include a hands-on activity in which each group uses a drone to present the route taken by their assigned fugitive slave. Students will identify landmarks and list the characteristics of each landmark along the route. Students will also use different colored pencils on a map to construct the various routes presented, and they will determine the amount of miles traveled on the journey to freedom. Writing a narrative of the assigned fugitive slave's journey to freedom will serve as the student assessment component of the lesson.

OBJECTIVE

- Construct an escape route for slaves to take on the Underground Railroad.

- Identify landmarks encountered and list the characteristics of each landmark.

- Use the scale on a map to determine how many miles were traveled.

- Write a narrative of a fugitive slave's journey to freedom.

MATERIALS

- Maps of North America (with scale; one for each group of students)

- Colored pencils (one set for each group)

- Large floor map of North America

- Rulers (one for each group)
- Drone

PROCEDURES

- The teacher gives a lesson on the Underground Railroad.
- Students identify slave states and free states.
- Students engage in a class discussion on the dangers of the journey and the consequences of being captured.
- The teacher assigns students to groups. Each group is assigned a fugitive slave to research. This research will include the slave's journey to freedom, and primary and secondary sources must be used.
- The teacher distributes the materials (maps of North America, colored pencils, and rulers) and assigns a group to each student. The groups are assigned the color that they will use on their map later on in the lesson.
- Each group uses their colored pencil to map out the escape route their assigned fugitive slave took on their journey to freedom.
- Groups identify the landmarks their slave encountered on the route and discuss the challenges they faced on their journey.
- Students use the scale on the map to determine the mileage traveled on the journey to freedom.
- Students demonstrate their understanding of the lesson by participating in a drone activity.
- An assessment concludes the lesson.

DRONE ACTIVITY

- The teacher lays out a large floor map of North America so each group of students can use a drone to map the journey to freedom of the slave they researched.
- On the map, a student places the drone on the starting location of the journey to freedom.

- The students in each group take turns navigating the drone according to the escape route of their slave, identifying and describing landmarks along the way (rivers they crossed or traveled near, cities they stopped in, etc.). After each landmark, a new student gets to navigate the drone to the next landmark. This continues until the end point of the journey to freedom is reached.

- As each group presents, the students in the other groups use their maps to construct the route being described, using a different color for each group's route.

ASSESSMENT

Students write a narrative of their assigned fugitive slave's journey to freedom.

MODIFICATION

The teacher assigns starting points for each group, and students map their own escape route.

- Group 1: Richmond, VA

- Group 2: Savannah, GA

- Group 3: Hagerstown, MD

- Group 4: Jackson, MI

ENRICHMENT

Students estimate how long the journey would take by car in the present day.

Extracurricular Applications

Drones have the ability to be used beyond just the general classroom. These uses may present either a primary use or a value-added element to provide the extra benefits needed to purchase a drone, especially a higher-end model for a school. The following are just some examples of how drones can be used beyond the classroom in a K–12 setting.

Communications and Video Editing

Drones are quickly becoming a commonly used tool in professional productions. It is hard to find a television show that has outdoor video without segments that were captured by a drone. Drones are the inexpensive alternative to production companies for obtaining footage that previously would have required aerial photography from a helicopter. The total purchase price of a drone can equate to one hour of operating time for a helicopter. Additionally, drones are able to go into places that a large aircraft may not fit or that could potentially endanger the crew. If a drone crashes, then it is just a small loss of money.

There is a growing demand for students who can operate a drone for reality TV, documentaries, and commercial applications. Just searching the phrase "drone" in one of the major job-search engines will provide numerous ads looking for drone camera operators for this type of application.

Using the drone for students to capture and edit video will provide them a skill set that they will be able to use beyond the classroom. The ability to capture dramatic shots where the drone is changing altitude and panning while maintaining a steady media capture is a high-level skill. Just as video-editing courses are geared to those who want to make a career path, mastery of the drone as a tool will enable students to open more opportunities. This is apparent beyond just television; industries such as real estate, insurance, and construction see the benefits of having drone footage.

Drones are not a course unto themselves but a tool that could be incorporated just as other cameras or editing software. Whether it be a student documentary, school news, sports footage, or a video project, drones can give a professional appearance at a rather low cost. And having this skill set will be something that students can carry with them for a lifetime.

Athletics

Sports teams have long used elevated platforms or lifts for recording practices and game footage. At ground level, the movement of players and development of a play has a limited vantage for a recording—players can block what is going on the opposite side of a field or course. But the use of a drone can enhance video recording even more than a lift or platform because the drone can hover over the field and move with the players. The knowledge of how players behave on the field is not only beneficial to coaches to enhance player performance but can be a matter of safety as well. If a player is performing in a way that may be hazardous to their own health or dangerous to other players, coaches can see this behavior on film and take appropriate action to correct it. Concussions have become a prominent issue in sports, for example, and there is a considerable amount of time and training going into developing ways to avoid concussions, such as proper blocking and tackling in football. Drones can capture the entire play development and allow coaches and staff to thoroughly train all individuals on the field. Some more-advanced models have the ability to recognize and track particular individuals, keeping pace with an athlete while they are performing.

Band

The ability to gain a high-altitude perspective is not only beneficial to athletics but to musical performances as well. Watching and recording the movement of students in choreographed performances is beneficial to increased accuracy and execution, especially as bands are trying to create particular shapes on the field. An aerial view allows directors to position and move band members more efficiently during drills and events alike.

Extracurricular Activities

PERSPECTIVES IN PHOTOGRAPHY

CONTENT

Art

ABSTRACT

This lesson concentrates on changing perspective through photography. The teacher will explain different perspectives in photography. Most photographs are taken from eye level. Changing perspective will make an immediate impact on photography. Getting the camera low can change how the viewer feels about the subject. Objects will appear much larger and more imposing. Getting the camera much higher than the subject will provide a sense of scale. Taking pictures laterally will change perspective. Drones provide various options for changing perspectives in photographs. Students will explore a subject by taking still photographs using a drone. Students will compare and contrast the different perspectives.

DRONE ACTIVITY

Flying a drone and capturing photographs of a subject.

- Students identify the subject they want to photograph.

- Students use the drone to take several photographs of the subject while hovering close to the ground, hovering laterally, and hovering very high above the subject. The drone is flown around the subject to take photographs at different angles. Students take turns flying and taking pictures with the drone.

- Students upload the photographs to the computer.

- Students compare and contrast the different9 perspectives of the photos.

BASKETBALL FORMATIONS

CONTENT

Physical Education

ABSTRACT

Being able to identify cues for shooting, rebounding, dribbling, and passing is necessary to successfully perform offensive strategies in basketball. These offensive strategies include the give and go, and the backdoor cut. The teacher uses a drone to record students playing basketball, then analyzes the video's formations and plays. Based on the teacher's findings, students receive guidance on how to use better strategies, as well as their athletic abilities, to become more successful within the sport.

DRONE ACTIVITY

- Half of the students align in formations on the basketball court.

- A student flies a drone over and around the basketball court while the remaining students run plays against those formations.

- The drone records the activity.

- The drone footage is shown to the students for the purpose of correcting their techniques.

BIRDSEYE JOURNALISM

CONTENT

Extracurricular Activity

ABSTRACT

Using drones in journalism widens the scope of an event from a human level to a bird's-eye view. This allows journalists a different perspective and truly captures the event. Students will use drones to cover a weather event as it is happening. For example, the drone could be sent out while it is raining to capture what is happening without exposing students to the elements. Students will then report on the event.

DRONE ACTIVITY

- The drone is flown outdoors around the vicinity of the school to record a weather event as it happens.

- Drone footage is transferred from the drone.

- Students edit the drone footage.

- Students report on what is seen on the drone footage. For example, students report on flooding in the street or snowplows clearing the parking lot.

FOOTBALL PRACTICE

CONTENT
Extracurricular Activity

ABSTRACT
Coaches can use drones to record team practices to gain advantages over their opponents. It is imperative for coaches to watch tape not only to improve the techniques of their own players but to prepare for future opponents. Coaches can mirror the formations and the plays of their opponents depending on what sport is being recorded. The advantage of using a drone over conventional ways of recording is that the angle of the video camera can be adjusted. Football stands out since these strategies have been embedded within the sport since its inception. The drone video allows coaches to see hand placement, the players' footing, and where the players have their eyes, among other things.

DRONE ACTIVITY
- A drone is flown around the football field.

- Coaches have some of the players line up in the upcoming opponents' formations.

- The remaining players then run their plays against those formations while the drone records footage.

- Coaches continue to alter formations to find which of their respective plays work best against the opponent's corresponding formations. The drone records all formations.

- Coaches go back to their film room and use the footage to develop a successful game plan.

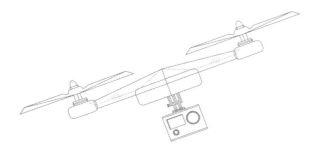

CHAPTER 7

Funding Opportunities

I n education, funds always seem to be limited when it comes to implementing new and creative innovations into a curriculum. This chapter will explore some of the alternative avenues that educators can use to obtain funding to purchase drones, but educators still need to ensure that they follow all laws and district policies when pursuing an alternative method for procurement.

Title I

Title I funding may be an option for qualifying schools when it comes to financing drones. Title I, Part A (Title I) of the Elementary and Secondary Education Act, as amended (ESEA), allocates financial funding to primary and secondary schools (Every Student Succeeds Act, 2015). Financial assistance is provided to local educational agencies (LEAs) and schools with high percentages of children from low-income families. The school must focus Title I services on those students who are at risk of failing to meet academic standards. A Title I school with at least 40% of students from low-income families can use the funds to operate a schoolwide program. This means Title I services can be provided to all students.

All costs associated with Title I must be "necessary, reasonable, allocable, and legal under state and local law" (Every Student Succeeds Act, 2015). Title I funds must be used to supplement not supplant educational programs and materials required by law (Every Student Succeeds Act, 2015). Title I funds can be used to purchase drones and drone-related services if the rationale proves that using drones for instruction is necessary to supplement teaching and learning in a core area. The following is a sample rationale for using drones in instruction.

> Schoolwide data shows a deficiency in mathematics, and students must be exposed to higher-order-thinking activities in order to help them prepare for the rigor of standardized assessments. Personalized instruction and interventions for at-risk students must be provided in order for these students to meet proficiency. Drones serve as a tool for remediation by (1) providing personal learning opportunities for students by differentiating activities; (2) supplementing skill-based instruction by encouraging collaboration and peer interaction while problem solving; (3) helping at-risk students by providing various interventions; and (4) modeling abstract concepts which then become concrete examples. Using drones in instruction promotes higher-order math conceptualization and understanding.

The Title I budget is broken into several accounts, with each account having a unique function and object code (Allison, Honegger, & Johnson, 2009).

Function/Code 100-600—Instructional Supplies Used by Students. Schools can purchase drones using this account. Other acceptable purchases include repair kits, batteries, and accessory kits.

Function/Code 200-300—Professional Development. Professional development designed to train teachers on the use of drones can be purchased using this account. Training teachers to operate drones is vital in the implementation of drones in any curriculum. Teachers need to not only be familiar with drone safety, rules, and regulations but comfortable in navigating drones in order to successfully engage students in drone activities. Training on how to implement the use of drones in instruction is necessary to achieve student success.

Function/Code 100-300—Vendors Contracted for Direct Instruction to Students. In order to use this account, the professional-development provider must work directly with the students. An example would be training the students to fly a drone.

Function/Code 400-731—Individual Items Valued at $2,000 or More. The purchase of a high-end, professional drone would fall into this category.

Title II

According to the Every Student Succeeds Act (2015), Title II, Part A is related to teachers and administrators, with the intention of improving student achievement by improving teacher quality. Allowable expenses are based on a needs assessment and must meet certain criteria. This criteria includes being aligned with state academic and achievement standards. To determine eligibility for using these funds to pay for drone-related expenses, a rationale as to how drones can be aligned with academic and achievement standards in at least one of the core content areas would have to be provided.

Title II, Part A is strictly for teacher resources. This includes professional development for teachers in core content areas. Materials related to the professional-development activities would be included—as long as they are for the teacher. For example, a drone for the teacher to model activities for the students would qualify. The device the teacher uses to control the drone (iPad, phone, etc.) would also qualify.

Crowdfunding

According to Forbes, crowdfunding is defined as "the practice of funding a project or venture by raising many small amounts of money from a large number of people, typically via the internet" (Prive, 2012). This is usually done using an online platform specific to crowdfunding, and the fees associated with crowdfunding sites vary. The fundraiser advertises the details of their project, including their financial goal and deadlines, and donors make contributions through the website, often receiving some form of recognition for their donation. There are many applications of crowdfunding, including education. Be sure to check with your school district before starting a crowdfunding campaign, as some districts prohibit teachers from participating. If your school district allows participation in crowdfunding campaigns, certain crowdfunding sites cater to education.

GoFundMe

GoFundMe is a crowdfunding platform that allows users to create a website to advertise and describe the project for the funding. GoFundMe has assisted their users in raising money for a wide variety of situations and events. A user would simply create a website as to why they are raising money to purchase drones for use in their classroom lessons. They would include their fundraising goal along with videos, pictures, and whatever else they feel will help raise money for their cause. Users then share their links via social media and email. The staff at GoFundMe reviews the campaign, and if the campaign qualifies, it will appear in the public search directory. Donors make their contributions through a secure website using a debit or credit card. As a fee, GoFundMe automatically deducts 5% from the donations the user receives.

DonorsChoose.org

DonorsChoose.org allows individuals to donate directly to a public school classroom project of their choice. Teachers create accounts and submit requests for materials and resources to complete their projects. Each project contains a line-item budget specifying the cost of the materials. A teacher with an account can request certain drones, batteries, repair kits, drone accessories, and materials for different activities; and a price would be specified for each item listed. Then DonorsChose.org purchases the materials and ships them to the teacher at the school once the listed price is collected.

Projects are searchable using a variety of options—school name, teacher name, location, content, material, and keywords—and donors give at least $1 to the project of their choice. Everyone who donates receives pictures of the projects and a letter from the teacher. Those who make donations of $50 or more get handwritten thank-you notes from the students. The fee for DonorsChoose.org is an optional 15% donation to cover overhead and maintenance.

There are many public, private, and nonprofit organizations that are willing to provide grants to fund drone projects in schools. Begin by checking the websites for the National Science Foundation, the United States Department of Agriculture, and the Department of Education.

As alternative methods for procuring money to fund educational materials and activities increase in popularity, it is important to consider existing policies that relate to nontraditional models, such as crowdfunding. Educators should consult with their school's legal counsel to ensure that they are adhering to the district's legal policies, procedures, and procurement practices. As with drone technology itself, fundraising is an area that has outpaced policies in many districts.

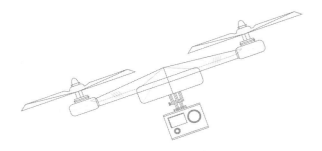

CHAPTER 8

Real-World Applications

The Federal Aviation Administration estimates that there will be 2.5 million drones in use in the United States by the end of 2016 with that number tripling to more than 7 million by 2020 (Meola, 2016). Drones are currently utilized in agriculture, filmmaking, conservation, search and rescue, military operations, and energy infrastructure. And Amazon announced in 2015 that it's working to develop Amazon Prime Air, a service that would use drones to deliver small packages to their consumers' doorsteps (Amazon, 2015).

While this has yet to become a reality, a cargo much more precious and valuable is already being delivered by giant quadcopters: humans! This new "drone taxi," named the Ehang 184, can carry a single passenger to a predetermined destination without a pilot at speeds of up to 62 miles an hour on a 23-minute flight (Hsu, 2016). The Chinese company EHang premiered the drone at the Consumer Electronics Show in Las Vegas in January 2016. It showed passengers using their tablets to set the destination information and clicking for takeoff and landing. The drone does the rest! With four arms and eight propellers, this megadrone is entirely electric and comes equipped with several safety systems in case of failure. The drone , according to Ehang, has a worldwide series of demo flights scheduled to begin soon. They also say the Ehang 184 should be commercially available this year with prices possibly in the $200,000 to $300,000 range.

There are many uses for these kinds of autonomous flying machines other than taxi service. The military is interested in using them for such missions as flying injured soldiers from a battlefield or delivering cargo. They are currently using the K-MAX unmanned cargo helicopter developed by Lockheed Martin and built by Kaman Aerospace; the drone has flown more than 1900 combat missions, delivering cargo for the U.S. Marine Corps. In addition, the Israeli company Tactical Robotics is developing an ambulance drone called the AirMule, which will be able to lift two wounded soldiers for a 31-mile trip. This use of drones in the military is a perfect example of utilizing robotic technology to save lives and avoid putting other lives in danger (Hsu, 2016).

If you have not heard about drone racing yet, you will soon. Drone racing is anticipated to be the next major global sport. Since 2014, there have been thousands of events held around the world. Over the next several years, this new sport is expected to attract millions of dollars in event sponsorship, broadcast rights, and profits in merchandise sales. Some estimates assert that the sport of drone racing will be a multibillion-dollar sport within the next 10 years.

According to AUVSI, the market for commercial drones is predicted to reach $82.1 billion by 2025. Currently, the development of drone technology costs an estimated $6.4 billion dollars a year (Dillow, 2013), and it is expected that drone technology will send data to the ever-expanding Internet of Things. Drones are being sent to Alaska to gather data for oil companies while CNN has been approved to use them for news gathering. Drones are also being utilized for precision agriculture, mining, security, and wildlife preservation; and as a result, drone jobs are abundant (Thompson, 2015). By 2025, there will be an expected 100,000 new drone-related jobs. Consider the utility of drones accompanying journalists, police officers, and home contractors to assist in these and many other professions.

In order to meet this demand for the workforce, many organizations are calling for STEM programs in K–12 and in higher education. Experimentation with drones in K–12 schools teaches students firsthand how drones can be useful in teaching, learning, research, and as a service to society. The National Science Foundation urges K–12 schools to incorporate engineering and STEM-related curricula in the precollege years. More STEM-trained students will be needed to secure the future of the United States as a leader in this area.

As technological advances continue across the globe, the introduction of STEM-based curricula in engineering and related content areas will help students succeed in meeting these needs. Ineffective K–12 STEM preparation is currently reflected in students' performance in college STEM courses. Many students are not choosing STEM-related majors when they enter college; more than 50% of science and engineering graduates from U.S. research universities are students from outside the United States according to the President's Council of Advisors on Science and Technology (Holden, Lander & Varmus, 2010).

The U.S. Bureau of Labor Statistics reports that in the next decade, many of the nation's fastest-growing jobs will be filled with employees who have a strong skill set in STEM-related academic areas. These jobs include computer and information research scientists, software developers, software engineers, and mathematicians. The computer and information research scientist occupation is expected to show a growth of 4100 jobs, or a 15% increase—a faster increase than the national average. For software developers, the bureau predicts that from 2012 to 2022 there will be an increase of 222,600 jobs, or a 22%

growth—much faster than the national average (U.S. Bureau of Labor Statistics, 2016).

Websites such as JobsinDrones.com and UAVCoach.com advertise hundreds of drone-related jobs each day. The descriptions range from drone camera operators for movies to licensed pilots to perform inspections of aerial towers. Based in Monrovia, California, AeroVironment is a company that makes small drones sold mostly to the military and used primarily to gather information. In 2016, the company hired 50 new employees and seeks to hire 50 more before the year is out.

References

Allison, G. S., Honegger, S. D., & Johnson, F. (2009). *Financial accounting for local and state school systems: 2009 edition* (NCES 2009-325). Washington, DC: National Center for Education Statistics, Institute of Education Sciences, U.S. Department of Education.

Amazon. (2015). Amazon Prime Air. www.amazon.com/b?node=8037720011

Brousseu, D. (2015). BCCAA bans drones at high school football games. SunSentinel. Retrieved from http://www.sun-sentinel.com/sports/highschool/football/broward/fl-high-school-notes-drones-banned-0819-20150818-story.html

Campanile, C. (2015, September 21). Most of NY's high-schoolers flunked Common Core algebra. *New York Post*. Retrieved from http://nypost.com/2015/09/21/most-of-nys-high-schoolers-flunked-common-core-algebra/

Carnahan, C. (2014). *The effects of learning in an online virtual environment on K–12 students* (Unpublished doctoral dissertation). Indiana University of Pennsylvania, Indiana, PA.

Cohen, D. (1967). A study of the efficiency of learning when both incidental and intentional learning occur simultaneously. *Final Report, 1*(1), 1–21.

Cook, B. (2015, May 6). North Carolina joins movement to ban drones at high school games. *Forbes*. Retrived from www.forbes.com/sites/bobcook/2015/05/06/north-carolina-joins-movement-to-ban-drones-at-high-school-games/#2c7ba70a48bf

Dede, C. (2015, November 23). A vision of STEM education in 2025. *EdTech Digest*. Retrieved from https://edtechdigest.wordpress.com/2015/11/23/a-vision-of-stem-education-in-2025/

Desilver, D. (2015, February 2). U.S. students improving—slowly—in math and science but still lagging internationally. Pew Research Center. Retrieved from http://www.pewresearch.org/fact-tank/2015/02/02/u-s-students-improving-slowly-in-math-and-science-but-still-lagging-internationally/

Dillow, C. (2013, March 12). What is the drone industry really worth? *Fortune*. Retrieved from http://fortune.com/2013/03/12/what-is-the-drone-industry-really-worth/

Erlichson, B. A. (2015, January). *NJ School Performance Reports – Interpretive Guide* (New Jersey, Department of Education). Retrieved from www.nj.gov/education/pr/1314/NJ School Performance Interpretive Guide 2015.pdf

Every Student Succeeds Act of 2015. Public Law 114–95., United States. Congress (114th, 1st session: 2015)

Felder, R. M. & Brent, R. (2009). Active learning: An introduction. *ASQ Higher Education Brief, 2*(4)

Gojak, L. (2013, December 3). "Algebra: Not 'if' but 'when.'" *President's Message*. National Council of Teachers of Mathematics. Retrieved from: http://www.nctm.org/News-and-Calendar/Messages-from-the-President/Archive/Linda-M_-Gojak/Algebra_-Not-_If_-but-_When_/

Guzman, A. & Nussbaum, M. (2009). Teaching competencies for technology integration in the classroom. 1(5), 453–469.

Higgins, S., Beauchamp, G., & Miller, D. (2007). Reviewing the literature on interactive whiteboards, *Learning, Media and Technology, 32*(3), 213–225.

Holdren, J., Lander, E., & Varmus, H. (2010). Prepare and inspire K–12 education in science, technology, engineering, and math (STEM) for America's future: Executive report. President's Council of Advisors on Science and Technology. Washington, D.C.: Executive Office of the President, President's Council of Advisors on Science and Technology.

International Society for Technology in Education. (2008). National educational technology standards for teachers. Retrieved from http://www.iste.org/standards/iste-standards/standards-for-teachers

Hsu, J. (2016, January 21). Drones aim to carry human lives. *Discover.* Retrieved from http://blogs.discovermagazine.com/lovesick-cyborg/2016/01/21/drones-aim-carry-human-lives/#.VwwSZVJ6JgI

Jarboe, G. (2015, November 06). Facebook Hits 8B Video Views Per Day, Challenges YouTube. Reelseo: *The Video Marketer's Guide.* Retrieved from http://www.reelseo.com/facebook-8-billion-video-views/

Kerka, S. (2000). Incidental learning. *Trends and Issues Alert* (18).

Konetes, G. (2011). *The effects of distance education and student involvement on incidental learning.* (Unpublished doctoral dissertation). Indiana University of Pennsylvania, Indiana, PA.

Langdon, D., McKittrick, G., Beede, D., Khan, B., & Doms. M. (2011). *STEM: Good jobs now and for the future.* (ESA Issue Brief #03-11). Washington, DC: U.S. Department of Commerce.

Loveless, T. (2008, September 22). "The misplaced math student: Lost in eigth-grade Algebra." *Brown Center Report on American Education.* The Brown Center at Brookings Institution. Retrieved from: http://www.brookings.edu/research/reports/2008/09/22-education-loveless

McFerrin, K. (1999). *Incidental learning in a higher-education, asynchronous, online, distance education course.* (Unpublished doctoral dissertation). Northwestern State University, Natchitoches, LA.

Meola, A. (2016, March 28). "Drone usage expected to triple by 2020." *Business Insider.* Retrieved from http://www.businessinsider.com/faa-says-drone-usage-will-triple-by-2020-2016-3

Murphy, J. and Roser, M. (2016). "Internet." Published online at *OurWorldinData.org* Retrieved from: https://ourworldindata.org/internet/ [Online Resource].

National Public Radio (Producer). (2015, November 19). *Chicago city council approves ban on drones.* [Interview transcript]. Retrieved from www.npr.org/2015/11/19/456600405/chicago-city-council-approves-ban-on-drones

New Jersey State Board of Education. (2015, November 4). *PARCC Results: Year One.* Retrieved from: http://www.state.nj.us/education/sboe/meetings/2015/November/public/SBOE%20PARCC%20Year%20One%20Results.pdf

New Jersey Department of Education. (2013). *New Jersey School Performance Reports—Interpretive Guide.* Trenton, NJ: New Jersey Department of Education.

O'Connor, A. (2015, July 29). Insurers warned to "think before you snap" as Florida drone privacy law takes flight. *Insurance Journal.* Retrived from http://www.insurancejournal.com/news/southeast/2015/07/29/376560.htm

Prive, T. (2012, November 27). What is crowdfunding and how does it benefit the economy. *Forbes.* Retrieved from http://www.forbes.com/sites/tanyaprive/2012/11/27/what-is-crowdfunding-and-how-does-it-benefit-the-economy/#689cc0e84ed4

Queally, J. (2016, January 20). L.A. city attorney files first criminal charges under new drone ordinance. *Los Angles Times.* Retrieved from www.latimes.com/local/lanow/la-me-ln-city-attorney-drones-20160120-story.html

RAND Mathematics Study Panel., & Ball, D. L. (2003). Mathematical proficiency for all students: Toward a strategic research and development program in mathematics education. Santa Monica, CA: RAND.

United States Department of Education. (1997). *Mathematics equals opportunity.* Washington, DC: U.S. Dept. of Education, Office of Educational Research and Improvement, Educational Resources Information Center. Retrieved from: http://files.eric.ed.gov/fulltext/ED415119.pdf

United States Department of Education. (2010, April 14). *Draft Proposed New Jersey Algebra I Core Content.* Retrieved from http://www.state.nj.us/education/archive/aps/cccs/math/alg1content.pdf

U.S. Bureau of Labor Statistics. (2016). U.S. Department of Labor, *Occupational Outlook Handbook, 2016–17 Edition,* Computer and Information Research Scientists,

Retrieved from http://www.bls.gov/ooh/computer-and-information-technology/computer-and-information-research-scientists.htm

Thompson, M. (2015, February 06). Jobs for drones are set to take off. CNBC. Retrieved from http://www.cnbc.com/2015/02/06/jobs-for-drones-are-set-to-take-off.html

Younes, M. N. & Asay, S. M. (2003). The world as a classroom: The impact of international study experiences on college students. *College Teaching, 51*(4), 141–147.

Policy for Drone Usage

POLICY FOR UNMANNED AIRCRAFT SYSTEMS (DRONE) USAGE

- All operation of drones on university property or by university staff/faculty must comply with FAA regulations and any laws of local, state, and federal governments. Any operation in violation of these laws is prohibited. The operator of the drone is responsible for compliance with all applicable laws.

- Usage must be for the purposes of research, training, or to support university functions.

- All operations should be conducted in a fashion that minimizes risks to other aircraft, property, and people.

- All drones should remain below 400 feet of altitude and be kept in visual sight of the person controlling the aircraft.

- The drone should not fly within five miles of an airport.

- The drone should not exceed 55 pounds in weight.

- Operating a drone outdoors should only be done during daylight during weather conditions that permit safe operation and control.

- When capturing images or video, the operator should ensure that they comply with all applicable laws and university policies regarding. The drone should not be used to record media in areas where there is a reasonable expectation of privacy.

- The use of a drone should comply with all other university policies.

APPENDIX B
Drone Safety Checklist

If you answer yes to any of the following four questions, complete the open-ended section below with a plan to operate safely:

- Are there trees present?

- Are there wires or antennas overhead?

- Will the drone fly over any people?

- Is there anything the drone could damage if it crashes?

If you answer no to these questions, take appropriate action to remedy the situation:

- Is the maximum altitude set to less than 400 feet?

- Do you have permission to operate on the property?

Do NOT fly if you answer yes to any of the following:

- Are there other aircraft nearby?

- Is there an airport within five miles?

Sketch out a plan to operate safely if you answered yes to questions 1–4:

_____

_____

_____

_____

_____

_____

_____

Drone Objective Sheet

Use this sheet to identify the objectives for your drone lesson and complete a storyboard that can be followed during the drone activity.

Topic of lesson:

Lesson objective(s):

Scene 1

Altitude:

Angle:

Speed:

Image or video duration:

Sketch the scene:

Scene 2

Altitude:

Angle:

Speed:

Image or video duration:

Sketch the scene:

Scene 3

Altitude:

Angle:

Speed:

Image or video duration:

Sketch the scene:

Scene 4

Altitude:

Angle:

Speed:

Image or video duration:

Sketch the scene: